Frank Cooke

GET TOGETHER

Teachers Assembly Book

Longman

Contents

Preface

This book was an afterthought!

Brenda Piper and I were discussing with Longman's music publishing editor the new hymn book for schools which she had commissioned us to compile: 'Now we need an assembly book to go with it,' she said. 'How about doing one, Frank?' Just as casually I agreed and all I can add is that it seemed a good idea at the time!

Professional schoolteachers will see my shortcomings and I can only appeal to their mercy. The aim is clear enough. It is to assist busy educators, called upon to lead assemblies regularly, by providing just a few more resource ideas for this bottomless pit of consumption.

Rosemary Dutton, my assistant, who typed all the manuscripts, listed the copyright permissions, and diligently and cheerfully worked on every word of this book, deserves far more than my brief but genuine public acknowledgement of deep gratitude.

Frank Cooke,
Andover, 1987

Longman Group UK Limited,
Longman House, Burnt Mill, Harlow,
Essex CM20 2JE, England
and Associated Companies throughout the world.

© Longman Group UK Limited 1987

First published 1987
ISBN 0 582 20614 6

Set in 11/13 point Palatino (Linotron)
Printed in Great Britain by Mackays of Chatham Ltd

How to use this book

This book is a do-it-yourself guide for all heads of school and others who are called upon regularly to lead school assemblies. It attempts to provide resource material for busy people who need all the help they can get. It may be used by itself or together with *'Get Together' Teachers Music Book* and *Students Assembly Book*.

It offers thirty themes, each of which begins where the young people are and attempts to stimulate responses by the use of music, poetry, prose, Bible readings (from the New International Version) and theology. Hymn numbers included here refer to those in the *Teachers Music Book*. A hymn index is included on pages 218–19.

It is intentional that far more material is provided for each unit than could be used in any one assembly. Selection is essential and is therefore a necessary part of the preparation.

The first part of each unit is for larger assemblies and contains two sections:

The Preparation section is addressed to the head or assembly taker and indicates the steps to be taken to lead that particular assembly effectively.

The Presentation section is addressed to the assembled school. This means it may be used as a script by the assembly leader and others invited to take part. Obviously each leader will adapt the text, making it his or her own. For example, the word 'greetings' which begins each presentation means the normal and natural greetings with which the leader would address the assembled school with or without school announcements.

Rehearse Preparation. Care taken in preparing an assembly always shows. Sensitive, clear reading is an education in itself.

The text refers you to extra material which is listed in the Contents, and to the final section of useful addresses.

1   An attitude of gratitude

For larger assemblies

Leader's preparation

1   Read through the presentation and select those items you intend to use.
2   Appoint the readers, giving them an opportunity to rehearse their items. If possible, give them a separate copy of their scripts.
3   Arrange for the hymns and musical accompaniment.
4   If possible and you think it is relevant, one or two pupils' personal stories could be used in this assembly, either read in essay form or conducted as a radio or TV interview.

THE SUBJECT
Any pupil who has (a) been rescued from some danger, or
                   (b) recovered from a serious accident or major surgery, or
                   (c) either himself, or a member of his family, had a remarkable escape of some sort.

THE METHOD
1   If you choose the essay method give the writer guidelines such as that the opening sentence should be something like 'I have real reason to be grateful because . . .', and end with something like 'This is why I am so thankful.'
2   Should you choose the media-type interview,
  (a) select as interviewer any member of the staff or senior forms who has a relaxed friendly manner and who will prepare relevant questions to draw out the story sensitively;
  (b) check that the interviewer has prepared a brief informative introduction, an opening and a closing question ('and finally one more question . . .'), and knows the exact time limit allowed for the interview;
  (c) decide if the participants are to remain 'on stage' or walk off afterwards, sitting down quickly.
3   Decide if it should be conducted seated or standing and if microphones are required, and arrange for the stage to be set well in advance.

Assembly presentation

LEADER   Greetings!
A minister used to visit a little invalid girl. She was a
devout Christian. One of her several sicknesses was a
tendency to curvature of the spine and she lived in a
Phelps' box. Have you ever seen a Phelps' box? It
looks like a shallow coffin and children with a
tendency to curvature of the spine used to be
strapped in one as nearly flat as possible. Her box
was by the window and she said to the minister one
day, 'In this position I can only look up. On the
nights I can't sleep I play with stars.' 'How can you
play with the stars?' he asked. 'I pick out the brightest
star and say, "That's Mummy", then another bright
star and say, "That's Daddy". I find a twinkling one
for my brother, my puppy, my spinal chair . . .' and
so on and on she went and concluded with this, 'But
there aren't enough stars to go round.'

Today our theme is an attitude of gratitude, giving
thanks, not taking anything for granted, but being
thankful. After all, it's not all that difficult – even a
dog will wag his tail. Let us give thanks to God for so
many things we enjoy.

Hymn number 86/28

LEADER   Now imagine that this is a broadcasting studio and
you are the audience at a 'chat show'. I'd like you to
meet your host who will introduce his guest(s) to
you. Please welcome . . .

INTERVIEWER   Thank you. My first guest this morning is . . . who
has quite a lot to be thankful for. (To his guest) Tell us
about . . .

LEADER OR
READER 1   Here is a true story told by the late Dr W. E. Sangster.
His friend the Reverend Professor William T. Stidger
was an American who wanted to thank somebody on
Thanksgiving Day. He began making a list of people
and things for which he was thankful and
remembered a lady who taught him in the Infant
School and first awakened his love of verse. He wrote
and thanked her. The reply was in a feeble scrawl and
began, 'My dear Willie' (he was now over fifty, bald

and a professor, and no one called him Willie any longer! It made him feel years younger).

My dear Willie,

I cannot tell you how much your note meant to me. I am in my eighties, living alone in a small room, cooking my own meals, lonely and, like the last leaf of autumn, lingering behind.

You will be interested to know that I taught in school for fifty years and yours is the first note of appreciation I have ever received. It came on a blue-cold morning and it cheered me as nothing has in many years.

The professor wept over it.

If *you* are grateful to anyone, say so, even if it's only 'Thanks, Mum'. Being thankful to God means showing gratitude to people.

READER 2   Let us pray.

In this prayer we shall think of some things for which we ought to be grateful. I'll pause after each one for you to say in your mind, 'Thank you, Lord'.

For health and strength and the gifts of seeing,
    hearing and enjoying so many good things,
For people who love us, care for us, even worry about
    us and want for us nothing but the best,
For the ones I love, for friends and all who mean a lot
    to me,
For music and laughter, reading and dancing,
    learning and sport,
For science and art, doctors and dentists, machines
    and gadgets,
For ordinary people who show courage and
    kindness,
For leaders, artists and those who uphold justice and
    protect us,
And especially now each one of us says 'Thank you'
    for one or two persons who are very important to
    each of us. *Amen.*

LEADER Here is a poem by Gerard Manley Hopkins, a modern English poet:

READER 1 Glory be to God for dappled things –
For skies of couple-colour as a brinded cow;
For rose-moles all in stipple upon trout that
 swim;

Fresh fire-coal chestnut-falls; finches' wings;
Landscape plotted and pieced – fold, fallow and
 plough;
And all trades, their gear and tackle and trim.

All things counter, original, spare, strange;
Whatever is fickle, freckled (who knows how?)
With swift, slow; sweet, sour; adazzle, dim;
He fathers-forth whose beauty is past change:
Praise him.

LEADER And now here is a marvellous list of things for which to be thankful, from the greatest hymn and prayer book ever written, the Book of Psalms. This one is Psalm 103 – try to count the good things the writer includes.

READER 1 Praise the Lord, O my soul; all my inmost being, praise his holy name.

READER 2 Praise the Lord, O my soul, and forget not all his benefits.

READER 1 He forgives all my sins and heals all my diseases;

READER 2 he redeems my life from the pit and crowns me with love and compassion.

READER 1 He satisfies my desires with good things, so that my youth is renewed like the eagle's.

READER 2 The Lord works righteousness and justice for all the oppressed.

READER 1 He made known his ways to Moses, his deeds to the people of Israel:

READER 2 The Lord is compassionate and gracious, slow to anger, abounding in love.

READER 1   He will not always accuse, nor will he harbour
his anger for ever;

READER 2   he does not treat us as our sins deserve or repay
us according to our iniquities.

READER 1   For as high as the heavens are above the earth, so
great is his love for those who fear him;

READER 2   as far as the east is from the west, so far has he
removed our transgressions from us.

READER 1   As a father has compassion on his children, so
the Lord has compassion on those who fear him;

READER 2   for he knows how we are formed, he remembers
that we are dust.

READER 1   As for man, his days are like grass, he flourishes
like a flower of the field;

READER 2   the wind blows over it and it is gone, and its
place remembers it no more.

READER 1   But from everlasting to everlasting the Lord's
love is with those who fear him, and his
righteousness with their children's children –

READER 2   with those who keep his covenant and remember
to obey his precepts.

READER 1   The Lord has established his throne in heaven,
and his kingdom rules over all.

READER 2   Praise the Lord, you his angels, you mighty ones
who do his bidding, who obey his word.

READER 1   Praise the Lord, all his heavenly hosts, you his
servants who do his will.

READER 2   Praise the Lord, all his works everywhere in his
dominion.
Praise the Lord, O my soul.   **(Psalm 103)**

Alternative New Testament reading

NARRATOR Now on his way to Jerusalem, Jesus travelled along the border between Samaria and Galilee. As he was going into a village, ten men who had leprosy met him. They stood at a distance and called out in a loud voice,

READERS 2
AND 3
(LEPERS'
VOICES) 'Jesus, Master, have pity on us!'

NARRATOR When he saw them, he said,

READER 4
(JESUS' VOICE) 'Go, show yourselves to the priests.'

NARRATOR And as they went, they were cleansed. One of them, when he saw he was healed, came back, praising God in a loud voice. He threw himself at Jesus' feet and thanked him – and he was a Samaritan. Jesus asked,

READER 4
(JESUS' VOICE) 'Were not all ten cleansed? Where are the other nine? Was no one found to return and give praise to God except this foreigner?'

NARRATOR Then he said to him,

READER 4
(JESUS' VOICE) 'Rise and go; your faith has made you well.'
(Luke 17:11–19)

LEADER *Only one* came back to say 'Thank you'.

And now a Thank You song.   (Solo, duet or hymn)

Hymn number 30/98/111

For smaller gatherings

Preparation

1 Select the appropriate items from the foregoing presentation, adapt them where necessary and arrange with those taking part to be fully briefed.
2 If you decide to use the TV interview approach then follow the preparations indicated and arrange for a rehearsal.

Additional ideas

1 Have the group discuss the benefits of writing 'Thank You' letters to people whom they may have taken for granted. When each one has a person in mind, allow them time to sketch out a letter in rough to be written and sent later that day.
2 Allow time for each child to write down a list of things for which he is thankful, followed by a brief discussion period in which good ways of expressing thanks can be raised, e.g. in word (by saying so) and in deed (saying thanks to Mum by doing the washing-up!).

Follow-up idea

For a further occasion on this theme encourage your group to put into their own words the General Thanksgiving and how best it can be used for thanksgiving prayers.

> Almighty God, Father of all mercies, we thine unworthy servants do give thee most humble and hearty thanks for all thy goodness and loving-kindness to us, and to all men. We bless thee for our creation, preservation, and all the blessings of this life; but above all, for thine inestimable love in the redemption of the world by our Lord Jesus Christ; for the means of grace, and for the hope of glory. And, we beseech thee, give us that due sense of all thy mercies, that our hearts may be unfeignedly thankful, and that we shew forth thy praise, not only with our lips, but in our lives; by giving up ourselves to thy service, and by walking before thee in holiness and righteousness all our days; through Jesus Christ our Lord, to whom with thee and the Holy Ghost, be all honour and glory, world without end. *Amen.*

2   The world and nature

For larger assemblies

Leader's preparation

1   Read through the presentation and select those items you intend to use.
2   Select the readers, arrange for rehearsal time and for the musical accompaniment.
3   Arrange for the taped music to be found, set and ready to fade in and out at the agreed signals. The opening music of '2001 – a Space Odyssey' is merely a suggestion. Many of the children will already have this, but unfortunately it is not now available from record shops but should be obtainable from most libraries.
4   Adapt and scale down Sir Fred Hoyle's model of the universe, convert measurements into metric equivalents and prepare pupils as your assistants. Take a little time to rehearse them to
    (a) go to agreed marked positions in and even beyond the hall as long as they remain in view;
    (b) carry and hold above their heads large cards indicating the planet they represent;
    or, if demonstrated on the platform, by using an orange to represent the sun, select points of reference in recognisable proximity to the platform, naming objects in the hall and beyond which would indicate the size and scale of the plan. A few moments adapting the model to your own premises is essential for effective communication.
5   If possible, obtain large posters and display them prominently, or obtain slides showing the galaxies in deep space, our own galaxy, the Milky Way and the earth photographed from the moon. Posters may be obtained from:
    The Royal Observatory, The British Astronomical Association, Madame Tussaud's and the London Planetarium, or from local poster shops.

Assembly presentation

LEADER   Greetings!
The theme of assembly today is Creation.
(Signal to fade in 2001 music, and gradually fade out as you say 'Let's do a scale model.' The team of children, prepared as indicated, take up their pre-

arranged places at the right distances, based on the following)

Let us represent the sun as a ball 6 inches in diameter. (This, by the way, is a reduction in scale of nearly 10,000,000,000.) Now, how far away are the planets from our ball? Not a few feet or one or two yards, as many people seem to imagine the solar system, but very much more. Mercury is about 7 yards away, Venus about 13, the earth 18, Mars 27, Jupiter 90, Saturn 170, Uranus about 350, Neptune 540 and Pluto 710 yards away. On this scale the earth is represented by a speck of dust and the nearest stars are about 2,000 miles away.*

When each child is holding up a planetary symbol, imagine him or her circling the 'sun'. The nearest sun to ours in our sun-packed galaxy, the Milky Way, on this scale is in Canada!
Here refer to the visual aids, explaining that our galaxy, the Milky Way, which we see end on, looks like this spiral M31 Ursa Major from the distance of a few million light years.
Here insert any other brief statements of your own explaining 'a light year', etc., and arrange the signal to fade in loudly, then turn down and run for a little while during the reading taped music from '2001 – a Space Odyssey'.

READER 1   In the beginning God created the heavens and the earth. Now the earth was formless and empty, darkness was over the surface of the deep, and the Spirit of God was hovering over the waters.
And God said, 'Let there be light', and there was light. God saw that the light was good, and he separated the light from the darkness. God called the light 'day' and the darkness he called 'night'. And there was evening, and there was morning – the first day.
And God said, 'Let there be an expanse between the waters to separate water from water.'
So God made the expanse and separated the water under the expanse from the water above it. And it

---

*From 'Nature of the Universe' by Fred Hoyle, published Penguin Books Ltd.

was so. God called the expanse 'sky'. And there was
evening, and there was morning – the second day.
And God said, 'Let the water under the sky be
gathered to one place, and let dry ground appear.'
And it was so.
God called the dry ground 'land', and the gathered
waters he called 'seas'. And God saw that it was
good.

(Genesis 1:1–10).

or

Where were you when I laid the earth's
foundation? Tell me, if you understand.
    Who marked off its dimensions? Surely you
know! Who stretched a measuring line across it?
    On what were its footings set, or who laid its
cornerstone – while the morning stars sang
together and all the angels shouted for joy?
    Who shut up the sea behind doors when it
burst forth from the womb,
when I made the clouds its garment and
wrapped it in thick darkness,
when I fixed limits for it and set its doors and
bars in place,
when I said, 'This far you may come and no
farther; here is where your proud waves halt'?

(Job 38:4–11)

or

O Lord, our Lord, how majestic is your name in
all the earth!
    You have set your glory above the heavens.
From the lips of children and infants you have
ordained praise because of your enemies, to
silence the foe and the avenger.
    When I consider your heavens, the work of
your fingers, the moon and the stars, which you
have set in place, what is man that you are
mindful of him, the son of man that you care for
him?
You made him a little lower than the heavenly
beings and crowned him with glory and honour.
    You made him ruler over the works of your

hands; you put everything under his feet:
all flocks and herds, and the beasts of the field,
the birds of the air, and the fish of the sea, all that
swim the paths of the seas.

O Lord, our Lord, how majestic is your name
in all the earth! **(Psalm 8)**

or

'To whom will you compare me? Or who is my
equal?' says the Holy One.
Lift your eyes and look to the heavens: Who
created all these? He who brings out the starry
host one by one, and calls them each by name.
Because of his great power and mighty strength,
not one of them is missing.

Why do you say, O Jacob, and complain, O
Israel, 'My way is hidden from the Lord; my
cause is disregarded by my God'?
Do you not know? Have you not heard? The
Lord is the everlasting God, the Creator of the
ends of the earth. He will not grow tired or
weary, and his understanding no one can
fathom.
He gives strength to the weary and increases the
power of the weak.
Even youths grow tired and weary, and young
men stumble and fall; but those who hope in the
Lord will renew their strength.
They will soar on wings like eagles; they will run
and not grow weary, they will walk and not be
faint. **(Isaiah 40:25−31)**

LEADER Hymn number 31/43/82 (or school choir)

LEADER Here is a poem by W. H. Carruth:

READER 2 A fire-mist and a planet,
A crystal and a cell,
A jelly-fish and a saurian,
And caves where the cave-men dwell;
Then a sense of law and beauty,
And a face turned from the clod –
Some call it Evolution,
And others call it God.

A haze on the far horizon,
An infinite tender sky,
The ripe rich tints of the cornfield,
And the wild geese sailing high;
And all over upland, and lowland,
The charm of the golden rod –
Some of us call it Beauty,
And others call it God.

Like tides on a crescent sea-beach,
When the moon is new and thin,
Into our hearts high yearnings
Come welling and surging in;
Come from the mystic ocean,
Whose rim no foot has trod –
Some of us call it Longing,
And others call it God.

A picket frozen on duty,
A mother starved for her brood,
Socrates drinking the hemlock,
And Jesus nailed to the wood;
And millions who, humble and nameless,
The straight, hard pathway trod –
Some call it Consecration,
And others call it God.

LEADER   Let us pray.

Invisible God, who made the vast mysterious
universe and everything in it, we are overawed by
the starry heavens above and the quiet voice within
us. We could never discover you by searching and
what we do know about you is because you have
shown yourself supremely to us in the life and person
of Jesus. We praise you for the glory of the arching
sky, the splendour of our planet earth, the lives of all
you have touched throughout history and for making
us with powers to think and see and hear, to love and
be loved, to enjoy so many of your wondrous gifts.
Lord, we praise you in your majesty and mystery.
Enable us to walk this earth with eyes opened to its
wonder and worth and to see beyond the sights the
mind and heart that made them. *Amen.*

Here is the last bit of a poem by Elizabeth Barrett Browning:

READER 1   nothing's small;
No lily, muffled hum of a summer bee,
But finds some coupling with the spinning stars;
No pebble at your foot, but proves a sphere;
No chaffinch, but implies the cherubim;
Earth's crammed with heaven,
And every common bush afire with God;
But only he who sees takes off his shoes,
The rest sit round it and pluck blackberries.

LEADER   Hymn number 100/110

For smaller gatherings

Preparation

1   Select the appropriate items from the foregoing presentation, adapt them where necessary and arrange with those taking part to be fully briefed.
2   Read through St Francis's hymn of praise, listing your own comments and points to raise in discussion.
3   Prepare, announce and explain your essay challenge, giving a deadline for handing it in and explaining that what they write would be confidential to you alone unless they were willing to share it with the class.

Additional ideas

1   Read together St Francis's hymn of praise:
    O most high Almighty good Lord God, to thee belong praise, glory, honour, and all blessing.
        Praised be my Lord God with all his creatures, and specially our brother the sun, who brings us the day, and who brings us the light; fair is he and shines with a very great splendour. O Lord, he signifies to us thee.
        Praised be my Lord for our sister the moon, and for the stars which he has set clear and lovely in heaven.
        Praised be my Lord for our brother the wind, and for air and cloud, calms and all weather by the which thou upholdest life in all creatures.

> Praised be my Lord for our sister the water, who is very serviceable unto us and humble and precious and clean.
>
> Praised be my Lord for our brother fire, through whom thou givest us light in the darkness: and he is bright and pleasant and very mighty and strong.
>
> Praised be my Lord for our sister the earth, the which doth sustain us and keep us and bringeth forth divers fruits – and flowers of many colours and grass.
>
> Praised be my Lord for all who pardon one another for his love's sake, and who endure weakness and tribulation; blessed are they who peaceably endure – for thou, O most highest, shall give them a crown.
>
> Praised be my Lord for our sister the death of the body, from which no man escapeth. Woe to him who dieth in mortal sin. Blessed are they who are found walking by thy most holy will, for the second death shall have no power to do them harm.
>
> Praise ye and bless the Lord, and give thanks unto him and serve him with great humility.

Now discuss together the way he sees nature in which even death is 'our sister'. Is all this too infantile for our day or has he seen something which completely escapes the scientific mind?

2 Prepare weeks ahead for this idea. Arrange an essay 'challenge' on the subject: 'Times when it was so beautiful I wanted to cry'. At an agreed date later *some* of the essays will be read by the writers without discussion or too much comment.

Follow-up ideas

1 Consider the possibility of arranging a visit to a planetarium after which the overall impressions of the group could become the basis of a discussion on this theme.

2 If possible, arrange for those interested to see the night sky through some friend's optical telescope.

3   Facing examinations

For larger assemblies

Leader's preparation

1   Read through all the items in the presentation below and select those
you intend to use.
2   Prepare the two scripts for the two readers 1 and 2 for the sketch.
Mark out the lines of each and rehearse them so that the interruptions
are natural and not stilted. Prepare them to wait and not to talk
through any laughter or sympathetic applause.
3   Arrange for readers 3 and 4 to have a copy of the text and time to
rehearse reading it; organise the accompaniment for the hymns.
4   Prepare the prayer leader if this is a different person from the
assembly leader.

ADDITIONAL POSSIBILITY
Several days ahead arrange for a small exhibition of certificates and
diplomas from staff and pupils which depict competence in swimming,
dancing, skating, driving, typing, etc., each exhibit certifying that the
holder has qualified in some skill or other. The Art Department might be
persuaded to set out the exhibition and prepare a poster announcing
something like 'School Achievements Recognised'.

Assembly presentation

LEADER   Greetings!
Next week we will be preoccupied with exams. The
fear of failure, of being asked questions for which we
are not prepared and the fear of not being able to do
our best, all crowd in on us and so often produce
'exam nerves'. We will concentrate on this today and
see if there is something helpful to be said about it.
We will begin with a hymn.

Hymn number 25/78

LEADER   Let's put exams into perspective. They are tests to see
if we have done the work, understood it and can say
or do something worth while with it. Let's eavesdrop
on a conversation that could take place anywhere
today.

SKETCH

READER 1   Exams are stupid. They don't really test what you know, only the bits you can remember at the time.

READER 2   Yes, sometimes it does seem like that but . . .

READER 1   I mean, I know some people who are brilliant at passing exams but who can't hit a ball, can't talk to a girl/boy without stammering and don't know how to enjoy themselves. Clever but stupid, you know what I mean?

READER 2   Yes, but supposing . . .

READER 1   Take history, for example, what blessed use is that to anyone?

READER 2   Well, it might be . . .

READER 1   And why memorise maths tables and stuff if you've got a calculator. Exams are a waste of time.

READER 2   Yes, but there is another . . .

READER 1   Think of all the people who failed all their exams who have made millions, and right duffers who won gold medals or became either millionaires or pop stars and there's the . . .

READER 2   Hey!

READER 1   What?

READER 2   Be quiet a minute because there's more to it than what you are saying. Suppose you fall down in a dead faint today and they rush you to the hospital, would it be bad for *them* to *examine* you?

READER 1   No, but come on, that's not the same as . . .

READER 2   Would you want to be anaesthetised and operated on by doctors who were clever but who had failed their medical exams, then nursed by nurses who were pretty but had never passed any nursing exams? Or would you want to watch football matches controlled by referees who had never been tested on the rules of the game?

READER 1   No, but that's not your book learning, is it?

READER 2   Much of it is, most of it is, but anyway, who said exams were about book learning? They are to test us as persons to see if we have benefited from the experience and errors of others who lived before us and so that we can learn to do the job better and better.

READER 1   Ah, but you're picking out the odd examples, aren't you?

READER 2   Am I? Do you want to get in a bus where the driver failed his passenger-carrying driving test, or a plane where the pilot never passed his landing tests, or send for a TV repair man who was only qualified with a pickaxe, or a teacher who had never learned to read?

READER 1   Some of them can't!

READER 2   Come off it! You know that exams are essential all through life, not just to see what you've learned nor what you can learn but to sort out those who can be trusted and those who can't!

(Both begin to talk at once – and are interrupted)

LEADER   Thank you – and there we break off the argument because, would you believe it, they both had points worth considering.

(The leader waits for readers 1 and 2 to sit down)

Listen to this.

READER 3   'I praise you, Father, Lord of heaven and earth, because you have hidden these things from the wise and learned, and revealed them to little children. Yes, Father, for this was your good pleasure.'   **(Luke 10:21)**

LEADER   And Paul the apostle, who was amongst other things one of the world's all-time academic geniuses, once wrote:

READER 4   For it is written: 'I will destroy the wisdom of the wise; the intelligence of the intelligent I will frustrate.' Where is the wise man? Where is the scholar? Where is the philosopher of this age?

Has not God made foolish the wisdom of the world? For since in the wisdom of God the world through its wisdom did not know him, God was pleased through the foolishness of what was preached to save those who believe.

(I Corinthians 1:19–21)

LEADER   Paul also said:

READER 3   Be very careful, then, how you live – not as unwise but as wise, making the most of every opportunity, because the days are evil. Therefore do not be foolish, but understand what the Lord's will is. Do not get drunk on wine, which leads to debauchery. Instead, be filled with the Spirit. Speak to one another with psalms, hymns and spiritual songs. Sing and make music in your heart to the Lord, always giving thanks to God the Father for everything, in the name of our Lord Jesus Christ.   **(Ephesians 5:15–20)**

LEADER   And again – pulling no punches – he says:

READER 4   Do not be deceived: God cannot be mocked. A man reaps what he sows. The one who sows to please his sinful nature, from that nature will reap destruction; the one who sows to please the Spirit, from the Spirit will reap eternal life. Let us not become weary in doing good, for at the proper time we will reap a harvest if we do not give up.   **(Galatians 6:7–9)**

LEADER   Now let us pray.

Dear Father God, we do not ask for fruits for which we have not laboured and dare not ask for rewards for that which has cost us naught. We do ask for desire to work while there is time, to offer only our very best and to be able to control our nerves, recall well what we have learned and rejoice in life's tests and trials which are meant to develop our spiritual and mental muscles.

We thank you for all who have worked hard to help us prepare for exams and thank you for all those who will encourage us to go on in life meeting the trials and tests with courage and fortitude. Through Jesus Christ our Lord. *Amen*.

Over and above all the things in which we are tested there is something else to consider.

READER 3   It was the late Bill Shankley, when he was manager of Liverpool Football Club, who said, 'Football's not a matter of life and death – it's more important than that!' He was speaking as a dedicated football manager. 'If you want to get on in this game', in other words, 'you have got to have skill, and in addition, total dedication – your attitude must be the commitment which says: it's more important than life and death.'

LEADER   Hymn number 119/131

For smaller gatherings

Preparation

1   Select the items from the foregoing presentation and prepare those who are to take part and rehearse them.
2   Give the group notice well ahead of time inviting them to bring with them any certificates, cups, shields, diplomas they or members of their family have won and tell them to be ready to explain what they had to do to obtain them.
3   Have the following ditty written up but out of sight until you are ready, or perhaps have a photocopy for each child, and let them punctuate it as a fun exercise:

> Caesar entered on his head
> A helmet on each foot
> A sandal in his hand he had
> His trusty sword to boot.

This will demonstrate the importance of what might seem a boring subject!

Additional idea

If the sketch printed in the presentation is enacted allow the group to continue the discussion, priming them with 'What do you think?'

4 Forgiveness

For larger assemblies

Leader's preparation

1 Read the material offered in the presentation below and select the items you intend to use.
2 If the Bible passage is to be read as a Scripture lesson pick the reader and suggest a rehearsal.
3 If you wish the reading to be dramatised, choose your characters, mark out their copies and rehearse them. They would need to read in character but not to learn their parts by heart. Six readers would be required: Narrator, Peter, Jesus, servant 1, servant 2 and the master.
4 Hymns. Check that the musical accompaniment is arranged and perhaps suggest one verse which may be sung unaccompanied.
5 Involve another member of staff to rehearse and then read the extract from Richard Weaver. It should not be read in an Oxford accent!

Assembly presentation

LEADER Greetings!
Today we focus on something so important that without it our personalities become shrivelled and warped. This is the subject of today's Bible reading.

NARRATOR Then Peter came to Jesus and asked,

PETER Lord, how many times shall I forgive my brother when he sins against me? Up to seven times?

NARRATOR Jesus answered,

JESUS I tell you, not seven times, but seventy-seven times.
Therefore, the kingdom of heaven is like a king who wanted to settle accounts with his servants. As he began the settlement, a man who owed him ten thousand talents was brought to him. Since he was not able to pay, the master ordered that he and his wife and his children and all that he had be sold to repay the debt.
The servant fell on his knees before him and begged,

SERVANT 1   Be patient with me and I will pay back everything.

JESUS   The servant's master took pity on him, cancelled the debt and let him go. But when that servant went out, he found one of his fellow servants who owed him a hundred denarii. He grabbed him and began to choke him.

SERVANT 1   Pay back what you owe me!

JESUS   His fellow servant fell to his knees and begged him.

SERVANT 2   Be patient with me, and I will pay you back.

JESUS   But he refused. Instead, he went off and had the man thrown into prison until he could pay the debt. When the other servants saw what had happened, they were greatly distressed and went and told their master everything that had happened. Then the master called the servant in.

MASTER   You wicked servant. I cancelled all that debt of yours because you begged me to. Shouldn't you have had mercy on your fellow servant just as I had on you?

NARRATOR   In anger his master turned him over to the jailers until he should pay back all he owed.

JESUS   This is how my heavenly Father will treat each of you unless you forgive your brother from your heart.   **(Matthew 18:21–35)**

LEADER   (Linking comment)
We need to forgive and to be forgiven if we are to be complete and healthy human beings. The trouble is, forgiveness is very costly. It is much easier to plan to get our own back but beware. Although 'revenge is sweet' it is a deadly poison which kills *us* and *our* relationships as well as hurting the ones we have not forgiven.

Listen to this true story of a coal miner called Richard Weaver who lived a long time ago.

READER   Weaver was a collier, a semi-professional pugilist in his younger days, who became a much beloved evangelist. Fighting, after drinking, seems to have been the sin to which he originally felt his flesh most perversely inclined. After his first conversion he had a backsliding, which consisted in pounding a man who had insulted a girl. Feeling that, having once fallen, he might as well be hanged for a sheep as for a lamb, he got drunk and went and broke the jaw of another man who had lately challenged him to fight and taunted him with cowardice for refusing as a Christian man – I mention these incidents to show how genuine a change of heart is implied in the later conduct which he describes as follows:

I went down to the drift and found the boy crying because a fellow-workman was trying to take the wagon from him by force. I said to him, 'Tom, you mustn't take that wagon.' He swore at me and called me a Methodist devil. I told him that God did not tell me to let him rob me. He cursed again and said he would push the wagon over me.

'Well,' I said, 'let us see whether the devil and thee are stronger than the Lord and me.'

And the Lord and I proving stronger than the devil and he, he had to get out of the way or the wagon would have gone over him. So I gave the wagon to the boy. Then said Tom: 'I've a good mind to smack thee on the face.'

'Well,' I said, 'if that will do thee any good thou canst do it.' So he struck me on the face. I turned the other cheek to him and said 'strike again'. He struck again and again, till he had struck me five times. I turned my cheek for the sixth stroke, but he turned away cursing. I shouted after him, 'The Lord forgive thee, for I do and the Lord save thee.'

This was on a Saturday; and when I went home from the coal-pit my wife saw my face was swollen and asked what was the matter with it. I said, 'I've been fighting, and I've given a man a good thrashing.'

She burst out weeping, and said, 'Oh Richard, what made you fight?' Then I told her all about it; and she thanked the Lord I had not struck back. But the Lord had struck and his blows have more effect than man's. Monday came. The devil began to tempt me, saying, 'The other men will laugh at thee for allowing Tom to treat thee as he did on Saturday.' I cried, 'Get thee behind me, Satan', and went on my way to the coal-pit.

Tom was the first man I saw. I said, 'Good morning', but got no reply. He went down first. When I got down, I was surprised to see him sitting on the wagon-road waiting for me. When I came to him he burst into tears and said, 'Richard, will you forgive me for striking you?'

'I have forgiven thee,' said I; 'ask God to forgive thee. The Lord bless thee.'

I gave him my hand and we went each to his work.

LEADER   Hymn number 12/88/10

LEADER   Forgive us, Lord, and break the pride which makes us put ourselves in the centre of every picture. Forgive our cowardice, our lying, our laziness, our lust. Forgive our greediness, our ingratitude and our never-ending supply of excuses, and show us how deeply our sins wound you. By your forgiveness, Lord, help us to forgive those who have made us feel small, hurt us, wounded our pride, stolen from us, laughed at us and lied about us, so that there are no grudges left in us, no hateful bitterness to poison us, and give us grace to pray for those who have wronged us. *Amen.*

The prayer I will now read was written by an unknown Jewish prisoner on a scrap of paper and left by the dead body of a child in the Nazi concentration camp of Ravensbrück.

O Lord, remember not only the men and women of good will, but also those of ill will. But do not remember all the suffering they have inflicted upon us; remember the fruits we have bought thanks to this suffering, our comradeship, our

loyalty, our humility, our courage, our
generosity, the greatness of heart which has
grown out of all this, and when they come to
judgment let all the fruits which we have borne
be their forgiveness.*

Hymn number 109/76

For smaller gatherings

Preparation

1   Select the appropriate items from the foregoing presentation, adapt
    them where necessary and arrange with those taking part to be fully
    briefed.
2   If you decide to turn Matthew 18:21–35 into a dramatic reading it will
    be necessary for the various characters to have copies of their
    speeches and also that of the narrator. Rehearse the reading with the
    children until it flows. Done this way the parable of Jesus becomes a
    play within a play and this may need to be explained to those taking
    part.

Additional ideas

Prepare a discussion on the subject of forgiveness. What does forgiving
our enemies involve? Use Matthew 5:43–45 as your starting-point and
invite answers and contributions on such items as
(a) Who are our personal enemies?
(b) Should we try to forgive them or not?
(c) Is it weakness to forgive?
(d) Can you forgive someone who isn't sorry?
(e) Does this apply to international disputes?
(f) Can you think of anyone you need to forgive?
(g) Can you think of anyone whom you need to ask for their
     forgiveness?

> You have heard that it was said, 'Love your neighbour and hate your
> enemy.' But I tell you, Love your enemies and pray for those who
> persecute you, that you may be sons of your Father in heaven. He
> causes his sun to rise on the evil and the good, and sends rain on the
> righteous and the unrighteous.   **(Matthew 5:43–45)**

*quoted by Mary Craig in 'Blessings', published by Hodder and Stoughton Ltd.

Follow-up ideas

1   Ask for volunteers to read *Tess of the d'Urbervilles* by Thomas Hardy and then to report back to the whole group on how the whole tragedy began at the wedding supper when, although she forgave her new husband, he refused to forgive her – for committing the same sin!

2   Discussion idea:
Remind the group of the story of *The Count of Monte Cristo* by Alexandre Dumas and let them discuss the power of revenge to motivate and to destroy. Perhaps a couple might volunteer to read the story and on a later occasion give a review of it to the group. The end of the story should not be neglected.

3   Using three columns on the blackboard, list
    (a) the things I need to forgive;
    (b) the things I need to be forgiven;
    (c) what to do about it.
Use the suggestions and discussion as a counselling session and perhaps even as a basis for prayer.

5 The passing of time

For larger assemblies

Leader's preparation

1 Read through the following presentation and select items you intend to use.
2 Arrange for two or more readers to read extracts, Scripture and prayers, and rehearse them.
3 Arrange for the musical accompaniment to the hymn.
4 The poem found in an old people's hospital ward calls for a good female reader who will rehearse the reading.

Assembly presentation

LEADER   Greetings!
The theme for today is summarised beautifully in words on an old clock in Chester Cathedral. Listen.

READER 1   When as a child I laughed and wept, Time crept,
When as a youth I waxed more bold, Time strolled,
When I became a full–grown man, Time ran,
When older still I daily grew, Time flew;
Soon I shall find in passing on, Time gone;
O Christ! wilt Thou have saved me then? *Amen.*

[Canon Henry Twells 1823–1900]

LEADER   Have you ever thought, when you were just about to go to the dentist's chair, or when you were going on holiday, or on Christmas Eve, 'The next time I think of this it will all be over'? Before you know it, it is! The exam you dreaded weeks ahead, the good time you longed for for months, had suddenly happened and is now past tense. Pondering this can make us feel a little sad and very fragile. Listen.

READER 2   Lord, you have been our dwelling-place throughout all generations.
Before the mountains were born or you brought forth the earth and the world, from everlasting to everlasting you are God.

You turn men back to dust, saying, 'Return to
dust, O sons of men.'
For a thousand years in your sight are like a day
that has just gone by, or like a watch in the night.
You sweep men away in the sleep of death; they
are like the new grass of the morning – though in
the morning it springs up new, by evening it is
dry and withered . . . .
Teach us to number our days aright, that we
may gain a heart of wisdom.   **(Psalm 90:1–6, 12)**

LEADER Now listen to part of an essay called 'How to live on
twenty-four hours a day' by Arnold Bennett.

READER 1 You wake up in the morning, and lo! your purse is
magically filled with twenty-four hours of the
unmanufactured tissue of the universe of your life! It
is yours. It is the most precious of possessions . . . . no
one can take it from you. It is unstealable. And no
one receives either more or less than you receive . . .
you cannot waste tomorrow; it is kept for you. You
cannot waste the next hour; it is kept for you. You
have to live on this twenty-four hours of daily time.
Out of it you have to spin health, pleasure, money,
content, respect, and the evolution of your immortal
soul.*

LEADER Hymn number 14/27

READERS 1
AND 2 Let us pray.

READER 1 Lord, help us to use today's time to do what we know
we ought to do, lest by leaving it, it is never done.

READER 2 Lord, teach us to take each moment as a space-gift
which we can fill with light for the dark soon comes
when no man can work.

READER 1 Lord, stop us deceiving ourselves saying, 'We have
no time' when we mean we don't want to do it
enough, and strengthen our will powers.

READER 2 Lord, your gift of time today is too precious to waste
by doing nothing worth while. Help us to use it all.
Amen.

*From 'How to live on 24 Hours a day' by Arnold Bennett, published Hodder and Stoughton Ltd.

LEADER A thought for today.
It's strange, but true – ponder it. Trying to make yourself happy is a waste of time. Try making someone else happy and discover your own happiness and that you have no regrets over the time spent on it.
Now here is some very old thinking on the subject. It was written centuries before Christ.

READER 1 There is a time for everything, and a season for every activity under heaven:
a time to be born and a time to die,
a time to plant and a time to uproot,
a time to kill and a time to heal,
a time to tear down and a time to build,
a time to weep and a time to laugh,
a time to mourn and a time to dance,
a time to scatter stones and a time to gather them,
a time to embrace and a time to refrain,
a time to search and a time to give up,
a time to keep and a time to throw away,
a time to tear and a time to mend,
a time to be silent and a time to speak,
a time to love and a time to hate,
a time for war and a time for peace . . . .
He has made everything beautiful in its time.
He has also set eternity in the hearts of men; yet they cannot fathom what God has done from beginning to end. **(Ecclesiastes 3:1–8, 11)**

LEADER He has also set eternity in the hearts of men – is that why we call time the 'enemy'?

Listen to these lines found in a locker in an old people's hospital ward.

FEMALE READER What do you see, tell me, what do you see?
Who are you seeing when looking at me?
A crabbit old woman, not very wise,
Uncertain of habit, with faraway eyes,
Who seems not to notice the things that you do,
And forever is losing a stocking or shoe?
Is that what you're thinking, is that what you
see?

Then open your eyes, for you're not seeing me.

I'll say who I am as I sit here so still,
As I rise at your bidding and eat at your will.
I'm a small child of ten with a father and mother,
Sisters and brothers who love one another;
A young girl of sixteen with wings on her feet,
Dreaming that soon her true sweetheart she'll
  meet;
A bride at just twenty, my heart gives a leap,
Remembering the vows I promised to keep.

At twenty-five I have bairns of my own,
Who need me to build a secure happy home.
A woman of thirty, my children grow fast,
Bound to each other with ties that should last.
At forty, my grown-up sons soon will be gone,
But my man stays beside me to see I don't
  mourn.
At fifty once more babies play round my knee,
Again we know children my loved one and me.

Dark days are upon me, my husband is dead;
I look at the future, I shudder with dread.
My children are busy with bairns of their own;
I think of the years and the love I have known.
I'm an old woman now, grace and vigour depart,
But thousands of memories live in my heart.
Inside it you see, a girl still dwells,
And now and again my tired heart swells.

LEADER   Hymn number 35/54

For smaller gatherings

Preparation

1   Select the appropriate items from the foregoing presentation, adapt
    them where necessary and arrange with those taking part to be fully
    briefed.
2   Arrange for a reader to read the Michel Quoist extracts.

        Lord, I have time
        I went out, Lord,

Men were coming out.
They were coming and going,
Walking and running.
Everything was rushing, cars, lorries, the street, the whole town.
Men were rushing not to waste time.
They were rushing after time,
To catch up with time,
To gain time.

Goodbye, sir, excuse me, I haven't time.
I'll come back, I can't wait, I haven't time.
I must end this letter – I haven't time.
I'd love to help you, but I haven't time.
I can't accept, having no time.
I can't think, I can't read, I'm swamped, I haven't time.
I'd like to pray, but I haven't time.

You understand, Lord, they simply haven't the time.
The child is playing, he hasn't time right now . . .
    Later on . . .
The schoolboy has his homework to do, he hasn't time . . .
    Later on . . .
The student has his courses, and so much work, he hasn't
  time . . .
    Later on . . .
The young man is at his sports, he hasn't time . . .
    Later on . . .
The young married man has his new house, he has to fix it up,
  he hasn't time . . .
    Later on . . .
The grandparents have their grandchildren, they haven't
  time . . .
    Later on . . .
They are ill, they have their treatments, they haven't time . . .
    Later on . . .
They are dying, they have no . . .
Too late! . . . They have no more time!
. . .
The hours are too short,
The days are too short,
Our lives are too short.
. . .

But we must not lose time
        waste time,
        kill time,
For time is a gift that you give us,
But a perishable gift,
A gift that does not keep.
                            (Pause)

Lord, I have time,
I have plenty of time,
All the time that you give me,
The years of my life,
The days of my years,
The hours of my days,
They are all mine.
Mine to fill, quietly, calmly,
But to fill completely, up to the brim.
To offer them to you, that of their insipid water
You may make a rich wine such as you made once in Cana of
   Galilee.

I am not asking you tonight, Lord, for time to do this and then
   that,
But your grace to do conscientiously, in the time that you give
   me, what you want me to do.

Follow-up ideas

1   Plan to show the Fact & Faith film on the relativity of time, as
     portrayed by the use of high- and low-speed cameras.
2   Ask for two or three volunteers each to read *Time and the Conways*, *An
     Inspector Calls*, *Dangerous Corner*, all by J. B. Priestley and all obtainable
     at most libraries. Use their findings to introduce a discussion at a later
     date on the subject of time.

6   Harvest

For larger assemblies

Leader's preparation

Long-term plans

It is worth making extra preparation *months* ahead for good Harvest assemblies.

The aim: To create a sense of gratitude and human solidarity which expresses itself in a giving and serving life-style.

The method: To make it easy for the children to respond practically to some of the needs presented.

Months ahead, in consultation, begin to plan a special Harvest week project by

1   Selecting your objectives (a small committee of older children may be formed for this purpose). There are so many, but consider one of the following:

   Save the Children
   OXFAM
   TEAR Fund
   Christian Aid

2   Deciding your strategy:
   Either do it all at school yourselves, or
   Invite a speaker from one of the agencies listed above, or
   Hire a film or video from one of the agencies or from one of the TV companies.
   In the presentation space is made for you to insert a 5/10–minute focus on the chosen appeal.
   Plan precisely what you expect the children to do as a result.

3   Literature. Have ready information for the children to take home and practical ideas if you expect them to do it themselves, with the bottom lines 'This is what you do now . . .', and tell them what response you hope for.

4   Obtain posters and/or a dozen or more overhead projection slides of rural scenes and a dozen or more of industrial scenes, shanty towns and airports, etc. Many such photographic slides might be obtained by means of a letter to parents requesting their use for the school assembly (see the opening of the presentation), or
   launch a poster competition in the school on the subject 'This is our world'.

Short-term plans

5 Read through the presentation and select those items you intend to use.

6 Choose at least three readers and rehearse them in their reading and prayers.

7 Arrange for the musical accompaniment to the hymns and if a film/tape introduction is used, the taped music of any suitably strong orchestral music. You may choose to leave the assembly to the taped music of 'Feed the world', Live Aid's fund-raising music (Polydor records).

8 Check that all the other arrangements are completed.

Assembly presentation

LEADER Greetings!
(Fade in tape of music to run under the introduction and then throughout the film/slide presentation.) Today's theme is the marvel of how God provides for our needs and how he expects the human race to share all the good things which are his gifts. (Draw attention to the posters displayed, or show slides on the overhead projector. These visual aids should create a variety of views of rural beauty and mountain grandeur, human slum and city skyline, cathedral, mosque and shanty town, airports, motorways and peasants with ox and plough, etc.)

Let us pray.

Let us give thanks to God for the daily miracle by which our lives are sustained:
for the heat of the sun,
for the good and fruitful earth,
for the changing seasons,
for the labour of men in field and factory,
for the traffic of men on land and sea,
for all in this and other lands by whose faithful labour we are fed and warmed and housed,
above all for him who came to share our lot, to live and work as man among men, to pour out his life for us and for all men, and to deliver us from sin and death, even Jesus Christ our Lord. With humble thankfulness, O God, we acknowledge thy mercy and thy love, and we offer unto thee again the devotion of our hearts. *Amen.*

Hymn number 85/21

READER 1   God has promised

READER 2   As long as the earth endures,
seedtime and harvest,
cold and heat,
summer and winter,
day and night
will never cease.   **(Genesis 8:22)**

READER 1   O Lord my God, you are very great; you are
clothed with splendour and majesty . . . .
He makes the clouds his chariot and rides on the
wings of the wind.
He makes winds his messengers, flames of fire
his servants.   **(Psalm 104:1b, 3b–4)**

READER 2   But at your rebuke the waters fled, at the sound
of your thunder they took to flight;
they flowed over the mountains, they went
down into the valleys, to the place you assigned
for them.   **(Psalm 104:7–8)**

READER 1   He makes springs pour water into the ravines; it
flows between the mountains.
They give water to all the beasts of the field;
the wild donkeys quench their thirst.
                               (Psalm 104:10–11)

READER 2   The birds of the air nest by the waters; they sing
among the branches . . . .
He makes grass grow for the cattle, and plants
for man to cultivate – bringing forth food from
the earth: **(Psalm 104: 12, 14)**

READER 1   wine that gladdens the heart of man, oil to make
his face shine, and bread that sustains his heart.
The trees of the Lord are well watered, the cedars
of Lebanon that he planted.   **(Psalm 104:15–16)**

READER 2   The moon marks off the seasons, and the sun
knows when to go down.
You bring darkness, it becomes night, and all the
beasts of the forest prowl.   **(Psalm 104:19–20)**

READER 1   The lions roar for their prey and seek their food
            from God.
            The sun rises, and they steal away; they return
            and lie down in their dens.   **(Psalm 104:21–22)**

READER 2   Then man goes out to his work, to his labour
            until evening.   **(Psalm 104:23)**

TOGETHER   How many are your works, O Lord! In wisdom
            you made them all; the earth is full of your
            creatures.   **(Psalm 104:24)**

READER 1   There is the sea, vast and spacious, teeming with
            creatures beyond number – living things both
            large and small.
            There the ships go to and fro, and the leviathan,
            which you formed to frolic there.   **(Psalm 104:25–26)**

READER 2   These all look to you to give them their food at
            the proper time.   **(Psalm 104:27)**

READER 1   When you give it to them, they gather it up;
            when you open your hand, they are satisfied
            with good things.   **(Psalm 104:28)**

READER 2   When you hide your face, they are terrified,
            when you take away their breath, they die and
            return to the dust.   **(Psalm 104:29)**

READER 1   When you send your Spirit, they are created, and
            you renew the face of the earth.   **(Psalm 104:30)**

TOGETHER   May the glory of the Lord endure for ever; may
            the Lord rejoice in his works.   **(Psalm 104:31)**

LEADER   Notice that the harvest is not merely a nature festival,
            but it includes also human nature. An essential part
            of God's harvest is the labour of men and women.

            Hymn number 132/34/61

LEADER   There has always been enough food for everyone on
            earth. The trouble is that we haven't learned how to
            share it.
            (More slides might be shown at this point from
            OXFAM or some other relief agency of Third World
            scenes of hunger, barrenness and need.)

READER 3   Imagine that all the population of the world were condensed to the size of one village of one hundred people. In this village, 67 of the 100 would be poor; the other 33 would be in varying degrees well off. Of the total population, only seven would be North Americans. The other 93 people would watch the 7 North Americans spend one half of all the money, eat one seventh of all the food, and use one half of all the bath-tubs.

These 7 people would have ten times more doctors than the other 93. Meanwhile, the 7 would continue to get more and more and the 93 less and less.

No matter where we live it is a blasphemy against God that while so many in the world's southern hemisphere die of starvation so many in the northern half die of diseases due to overeating.

[David Watson]

(At this point, introduce the school's chosen and prepared effort to raise money for a special project in the Third World, either by
(a) reading the information sent to you, or
(b) introducing the speaker from the relief agency to describe the need and what can be done to help, or by
(c) showing a short video of that Third World need.)

LEADER   It is an emergency task to send aid to feed the starving. The long-term task is in making every country capable of feeding its own people. That is the job of government, trade, industry, science, commerce, agriculture, engineering, electronics, the building and transport industries, in fact, the whole skill of the human race pulling together is needed to feed the world. Every one of us has a part in that great plan. Let us pray. (Prayer for two readers)

READER 1   Our Father, who art in heaven.

READER 2   You are our Father and the Father of all other men and women, boys and girls too, well-fed and hungry alike.

READER 1   Hallowed be thy name.

READER 2 In the fairer sharing of our wealth, in caring for the unprotected and the underprivileged, let your name be honoured.

READER 1 Thy kingdom come. Thy will be done on earth as in heaven.

READER 2 Your rule be seen in the affection we show, the honesty we adopt, the way we share the good things of life as individuals and as a school and as a nation.

READER 1 Give us this day our daily bread.

READER 2 Food for our bodies, our minds, our spirits to sustain us, to inspire us and to empower us, and for all the world's people.

READER 1 Forgive us our trespasses as we forgive those who trespass against us.

READER 2 Set us free from our guilt and help us forgive all who have hurt us and put right some of the damage today.

READER 1 Lead us not into temptation.

READER 2 Instead give us courage to cast out our cowardice, love to cast out fear and give us self-control that silences the inner voice which continually cries 'I want, I want'.

READER 1 Deliver us from the evil one.

READER 2 From satanic destruction, of violence and hatred, of sheer wanton wickedness, cynicism and despair, deliver us.

READER 1 For thine is the kingdom, the power and the glory, for ever and ever.

READER 2 You are the only true King and the only one humble enough to receive praise and to exercise power, and we worship you.

TOGETHER *Amen.*

LEADER Hymn number 31/48/59

For smaller gatherings

Preparation

1 Select the appropriate items from the foregoing presentation, adapt them where necessary, and arrange that those taking part are fully briefed.
2 Obtain posters from relief agencies listed in the larger assembly presentation and from local travel agents. Arrange also for the display to be set up and later taken down.
3 Book a speaker from International Boys Town Trust, India, or from one of the agencies listed in the leader's preparation for the larger assemblies in this unit.

Additional ideas

1 Plan well ahead for a group to work out where every item that could be found on any breakfast table originated, for example, tea from India, coffee from Brazil, sugar from the West Indies, etc., and don't forget the cloth and the salt and pepper and the cutlery.
   On the day they could begin with a bare table and set it item by item while someone listed the countries concerned.
2 Parable of the talents *now*. Arranging well ahead, find some charity, individual or Rotary Club willing to give to the children (working in pairs) a small sum of money for them to use in some way in order to make it grow for the charity concerned. Launch the project by reading:

> Again, it will be like a man going on a journey, who called his servants and entrusted his property to them. To one he gave five talents of money, to another two talents, and to another one talent, each according to his ability. Then he went on his journey. The man who had received the five talents went at once and put his money to work and gained five more. So also, the one with the two talents gained two more. But the man who had received the one talent went off, dug a hole in the ground and hid his master's money.
>
> After a long time the master of those servants returned and settled accounts with them. The man who had received the five talents brought the other five. 'Master,' he said, 'you entrusted me with five talents. See, I have gained five more.'
>
> His master replied, 'Well done, good and faithful servant! You have been faithful with a few things; I will put you in charge of many things. Come and share your master's happiness!'

The man with the two talents also came. 'Master,' he said, 'you entrusted me with two talents; see, I have gained two more.'

His master replied, 'Well done, good and faithful servant! You have been faithful with a few things; I will put you in charge of many things. Come and share your master's happiness!'

Then the man who had received the one talent came. 'Master,' he said, 'I knew that you are a hard man, harvesting where you have not sown and gathering where you have not scattered seed. So I was afraid and went out and hid your talent in the ground. See, here is what belongs to you.'

His master replied, 'You wicked, lazy servant! So you knew that I harvest where I have not sown and gather where I have not scattered seed? Well then, you should have put my money on deposit with the bankers, so that when I returned I would have received it back with interest.'   **(Matthew 25:14–27)**

Explain that the story teaches that you lose what you do not use and gain by putting what you have to use.

Then distribute the information and deal with any questions such as opening and closing dates and guidelines.

Have a special starting day and finishing day occasion and a presentation event. Adapt these ideas to your situation.

3   Have an old-fashioned 'Give and Take', where the children bring suitable food gifts and distribute them among the needy in the area surrounding the school. (Names can be obtained from local churches, local Age Concern group, social workers, Round Table and Rotary, etc.)

Follow-up ideas

1   A number of the suggestions in this unit have automatic follow-up in that, for example, in the Boys Town (India) project, the 'boy' adopted writes a quarterly newsletter keeping everyone interested in touch with his progress.

2   Remember to pray regularly for the needy, the hungry and the homeless and for the relief workers who do all they can to help.

7 Prayer

For larger assemblies

Leader's preparation

1 Read through the presentation and select those items you intend to use.
2 Find a good 'actor' amongst the senior children for the first sketch, plus a table and a telephone as a prop. Provide the 'actor' with a copy of the script and insist on adequate rehearsal. A microphone will almost certainly be required.
3 Ask the Art Department to paint or chalk up a huge hand (or use a large print of 'Praying Hands').
4 Arrange for a helper who will print the appropriate letter on each finger (and thumb) as you come to it:

S   T   O   A   L

5 Rehearse the demonstration. You may wish to add to the brief explanation provided.
6 Arrange for a reader for the poem on prayer.
7 The story 'The White Birds' by Olive Wyon is a long item but it should be performed in total at an assembly where time has been allowed for it, or be abbreviated and used as an item in an assembly on prayer.

    It can be read as a story by one reader or in three parts: the narrator, the man and the angel. Preparation should be made and time allowed for its rehearsal.
8 Arrange for the musical accompaniment for the hymns.

Assembly presentation

LEADER   Greetings!
            The theme for today's assembly is a mysterious means of communication – of talking and listening – but it is not quite as simple as using a telephone. It is called Prayer. Listen

READER 1   (using a stage prop telephone, spelling out the letters and numbers) P S A L M 3 0 1 8 1 0
            Hello, is that you, Lord? Yes, I'm sorry, I meant to ring earlier this week, but you know how it is. I got interested in TV and . . . yes, I did fall asleep

watching . . . I'm sorry because I wanted to explain that I'd called your number five times last week but the line was dead. I wondered . . . what's that, Lord? Yes . . . I had had that row with John and I did say I'd never forgive him, and that I hated his guts. What's that got to do with my not getting through to you . . .? (Pause) OK, I see . . . your line often goes dead when we try to phone you while we are hating and fuming and stewing to get our own back . . . still, I told him I was sorry and made it up with him and immediately I dialled your number I got through . . . I'm sorry, Lord, that I am a bit of an idiot at times . . . I said at times, Lord. What's the joke? All right, Lord, thanks for everything. You're great!

LEADER   There are many different kinds of praying. Let's look at some. (Reveal the picture of a huge hand.) Here is a simple handful of prayer! Each digit has a letter to denote a different kind of praying:

The S stands for *sorry prayers*. This is when we own up and apologise to God and ask to put things right. This is called confession of our sin.

The T stands for *thank you prayers*. Here we say thanks to God for so many things we so often take for granted – think of some now. Our senses, our health, people who love us and whom we love, our food, our clothing, our homes, etc.

The O stands for *others*. Think of some people you need to lift up and imagine God pouring love and healing on them. Just picture them now as they are and imagine God touching them and giving them what they need. Name someone quietly in your thoughts.

The A stands for *asking prayers*. Jesus said we should ask our heavenly Father for what we need but remember you can be too selfish! Don't think 'what would I like' but 'what do I really need'. Go on then if you dare – ask for it!

The L stands for *listening prayers*, when you become still and listen to the quiet voice of the Lord speaking directly into your thoughts.

To pray like this for just a moment on each of these is quite a handful of real prayer.

Let's try an experiment
(a) Relax, now be still, close your eyes. Breathe deeply and slowly, don't lift your shoulders. Let all your muscles go limp. Now think and give thanks for just one moment in silence.
(b) Open your eyes and still relaxed listen to this prayer from the greatest hymn and prayer book in the world called the Book of Psalms.

READER 2　Lord, who may dwell in your sanctuary?
Who may live on your holy hill?
He whose walk is blameless and who does what is righteous, who speaks the truth from his heart and has no slander on his tongue,
who does his neighbour no wrong and casts no slur on his fellow man,
who despises a vile man but honours those who fear the Lord,
who keeps his oath even when it hurts,
who lends his money without usury and does not accept a bribe against the innocent.
He who does these things will never be shaken.
(Psalm 15)

LEADER　Hymn number 95/107

Now, a 4,000-year-old prayer:

The Lord bless you and keep you,
the Lord make his face shine upon you and be gracious to you;
the Lord turn his face towards you and give you peace.　**(Numbers 6:24–26)**

Does God always answer prayer?
Yes, but sometimes he says 'Yes',
　　　sometimes he says 'No'
　　　and sometimes he says 'Wait'.

Listen to this.

READER 3　I asked God for strength, that I might do greater things,
I was made weak, that I might learn humbly to obey . . .

I asked for health, that I might do greater things,
I was given infirmity, that I might do better
things . . .
I asked for riches, that I might be happy,
I was given poverty, that I might be wise . . .
I asked for power, that I might have the praise of
men,
I was given weakness, that I might feel the need
of God . . .
I asked for all things, that I might enjoy life,
I was given life, that I might enjoy all things . . .
I got nothing that I asked for, but everything I
had hoped for,
Almost despite myself, my unspoken prayers
were answered,
I am among all men, most richly blessed.

These words of an unknown Confederate soldier can
be seen cast in bronze in the lobby of the Institute of
Physical Medicine and Rehabilitation in New York
City.

LEADER   This is the Story of the White Birds:

READER 1
(or read in three
parts)
   There was once a man who had a waking dream. He
dreamed he was in a spacious church. He had
wandered in to pray, and after his prayers were
finished, he knelt on, his eyes open, gazing round at
the beauty of the ancient building, and resting in the
silence. Here and there in the great building were
quiet kneeling figures. Across the dim darkness of
the nave and aisles shafts of sunlight streamed into
the church from upper windows. In the distance a
side door was open, letting in scents of summer air,
fragrant with the smell of hay and flowers, and the
sight of trees waving in the breeze, and beyond, a
line of blue hills, dim and distant as an enchanted
land.

     Presently the man withdrew his eyes from the
pleasant outdoor world and looked again at the
church. Suddenly, close to the spot where he was
kneeling, there was a gentle whir of wings and he
saw a little white bird fluttering about in the dim
nave; it flew uncertainly hither and thither, and once

or twice he thought it would fall to the ground. But gradually it gathered strength, rose towards the roof, and finally, with a purposeful sweep of its wings, sped upwards, and out through one of the open windows into the sunshine.

The stranger looked down again at the kneeling men and women, scattered singly throughout the building; and now he saw what he had not noticed before: that by the side of each worshipper there hovered, close to the stone floor, a little white bird. Just then he saw another bird rise from the floor and try to reach the roof. But it, too, was in difficulties; it flew round and round in circles, occasionally beating its wings in a futile way against the great lower windows, rich with stained glass. Finally it sank down exhausted, and lay still. A little later another bird rose from the ground, with a swift and easy flight; for a moment it seemed that it would reach the open window and the open air beyond; but suddenly, it whirled round, fell helplessly over and over, and came to the ground with a thud, as if it had been shot. The man rose from his knees and went over to see what had happened; the little bird was dead.

He went back to his place and sat down on one of the chairs; then he noticed an ugly little bird, its white feathers dirty and bedraggled, rise from the ground. At first this bird laboured heavily, but it soon gathered speed, for it was strong, and it soared up and out into the sunlit world beyond the walls of the great church. More and more the man wondered what all this might mean? He looked again at the persons at prayer near him, and he noticed one, kneeling very reverently, by whose side lay a very beautiful bird, snowy white and perfectly formed. But when he looked at it more closely he saw that its eyes were glazed, its wings stiff; it was a lifeless shell. 'What a pity!' he murmured under his breath. At that moment, a gentle whir of wings a few feet away attracted his attention: another bird was rising from the ground, steadily and quietly, at first with some appearance of effort, but more and more easily and lightly as it gathered strength; this bird flew straight

up, past the carved angels which seemed to be crying
'Hallelujah!' to one another across the dim spaces of
the church, and out through the open window into
the blue sky, where it was soon lost to sight.

Pondering on what he had seen, the man looked
round again, and this time he saw standing close to
him, an angel, tall and strong, with a face of great
kindness, wisdom and compassion. It all seemed
perfectly natural (as things do in dreams), and the
man whispered to him, 'Can you explain to me about
these white birds?'

'Yes,' said the angel, in a low voice, as he seated
himself beside him, 'for I am the guardian of this
place of prayer. These white birds are the outward
sign of the prayers of the people who come here to
pray. The first bird, which found it difficult to rise,
but then succeeded, is the prayer of a woman who
has come here straight from a very busy life; she has
very little time to herself; in fact she usually comes
here in the midst of her shopping. She has a great
many duties and claims, and her mind was full of
distractions when she first knelt down and tried to
pray. But she persevered, for her heart is right with
God, and he helped her; her prayer was real and her
will good, so her prayer reached God.' 'And what
about the bird that flew round in circles?' asked the
man. The angel smiled slightly, with a tinge of faint
amusement. 'That,' he said slowly, 'is the prayer of a
man who thinks of no one but himself; even in his
prayers he only asks for 'things' – success in his
business and things like that; he tries to use God for
his own ends . . . people think he is a very religious
man . . . but his prayer does not reach God at all.'

'But why did that other bird fall to the ground as if
it had been shot?' The angel looked sad as he replied:
'That man began his prayer well enough; but
suddenly remembered a grudge against someone he
knew; he forgot his prayer and brooded in bitter
resentment, and his bitterness killed his prayer. . . .
And the ugly little bird,' he went on after a moment's
silence, 'is the prayer of a man who hasn't much idea
of reverence; his prayer is bold, almost
presumptuous, some people might call it; but God

knows his heart, and he sees that his faith is real; he does really believe in God, so his prayer reaches him.'

'And the beautiful lifeless bird that never stirred from the ground at all?' said the man. 'That,' said the angel, 'is a beautifully composed prayer; the language is perfect, the thought is doctrinally correct; the man offered it with the greatest solemnity and outward reverence . . . . But he never meant a word of it; even as he said the words his thoughts were on his own affairs; so his prayer could not reach God.'

'And what about the last bird that flew upwards so easily?' The angel smiled. 'I think you know,' he said gently. 'That is the prayer of a woman whose whole heart and will is set upon God . . . . Her prayer went straight to God.'

LEADER   Hymn number 116/117

For smaller gatherings

Preparation

1   Select the appropriate items from the foregoing presentation, adapt them where necessary and arrange with those taking part to be fully briefed.
2   Ahead of time warn your group that you are going to ask for any answers to prayer which they believe have happened to them. If you have one of your own, be ready with it.
3   Ask for two reliable volunteers to prepare in their own words the various items of the Lord's Prayer from Matthew 6:9–13.
    Ask them to 'fill out' what they think each petition means. You may find it helpful to refer to page 36 of the Harvest presentation where the Lord's Prayer is expanded.

Additional ideas

In one of his many helpful books Dr Roger Pilkington tells of an experience which happened to him some years ago. He had gone to South Wales to give a series of lectures in a postgraduate biology course. Through a succession of unforeseen events he was forced to change his hotel. When he finally arrived at the place where he was to stay for the night, a tired-looking and pale middle-aged receptionist greeted him.

'We can only get you a cold supper,' she said. 'But if you come into the office any time after nine o'clock you can have a cup of tea.'

Dr Pilkington lectured that evening and, when he returned to the hotel, he decided to accept the offer of a cup of tea. He found the receptionist chatting with two commercial travellers and discussing, oddly enough, the question of suicide. Thinking him a medical doctor, she asked him if he thought that people who put their heads in a gas oven suffered a lot of pain. She also asked if he knew how many aspirin tablets would make up a lethal dose. The conversation switched to less morbid subjects, and Dr Pilkington, finishing his tea, went to bed.

But he could not sleep. He had been lying wide awake in bed for a few moments when a feeling came over him which he describes as 'a sense of being charged like a condenser'. Throwing on his dressing-gown, he ran down four flights of stairs, walked straight into the inner office, confronted the receptionist and asked bluntly, 'I want to know why you are going to commit suicide.' She began to protest, but Dr Pilkington cut her short. 'I know you're going to. I shall not stop you. But you must tell me *why* you are going to do it.'

The woman broke down and told him her story. At the age of forty-three her father had become totally blind, and she, who was now approaching her forty-third birthday, had been told in all sincerity by the family doctor that the disease was hereditary. Unable to face the thought of a lonely spinsterhood of helpless blindness, she had decided to opt out of life by committing suicide. It happened that in those days Dr Pilkington was a geneticist and that he had been working on eye defects in animals and had also made a particular study of the inheritance of faults of vision in humans. The receptionist had only to describe her father's condition in the barest outline for him to see at once that it was not hereditary. He convinced her of this beyond a shadow of a doubt. 'You can go back to bed,' she said. 'I know you are not deceiving me. Don't worry. I shall not kill myself tonight or ever.' She also told him that every day since consulting her doctor she had prayed the same prayer: 'Please God, show me how I can kill myself and put an end to it all.'

Follow-up idea

GROUP EXPERIMENT

Write down the names of a personal friend, an enemy, a relative, and privately pray for each one each day for the next two weeks for their well-being and then honestly say if anything has changed.

8   The mysterious presence

For larger assemblies

Leader's preparation

1   Read through the presentation and select those items you intend to use.
2   Arrange for two good dramatic readers, either members of staff or gifted senior scholars. Provide copies of the text they are to read.
3   Arrange for amplification and rehearsal.
4   Arrange for the musical accompaniment to the hymns.

Assembly presentation

LEADER   Greetings!
Hymn number 136/47
Today's theme is very hard to explain but is one which that hymn opened up and which some of you will recognise at once.

   It is the strange feeling people sometimes have that beyond what they can see or touch or hear they become aware of a power, a presence which is awesome, yet good, and which is not an 'it' but an invisible 'person' communicating with them. The experience may not last long and cannot be stage-managed or arranged by us, yet it makes a permanent mark, and ever after we know it was real. Listen.

READER 1   I had spent the evening in a great city, with two friends, reading and discussing. I had a long drive to my lodging. I was in a state of quiet, almost passive enjoyment. All at once, without warning of any kind, I found myself wrapped in a flame-coloured cloud. For an instant I thought of fire, an immense conflagration somewhere close by in that great city; the next, I knew that the fire was within myself. Directly afterward there came upon me a sense of exultation, of immense joyousness accompanied or immediately followed by an intellectual illumination impossible to describe. Among other things, I did not merely come to believe, but I saw that the universe is not composed of dead matter, but is, on the contrary, a living Presence; I became conscious in myself of eternal life. It was not a conviction that I would have eternal life, but a consciousness that I possessed eternal life then. The vision lasted a few seconds and was gone; but the memory of it, the reality of what it wrought has remained during the quarter of a century which has since elapsed. That view, that conviction, has never, even during periods of the deepest depression, been lost.

LEADER   There you have a description of one of those mysterious life-changing experiences as told by a Canadian Psychiatrist called R. M. Bucke. Here are some extracts from the Bible. The first is from the Book of Exodus.

READER 2   Now Moses was tending the flock of Jethro his father-in-law, the priest of Midian, and he led the flock to the far side of the desert and came to Horeb, the mountain of God. There the angel of the Lord appeared to him in flames of fire from within a bush. Moses saw that though the bush was on fire it did not burn up. So Moses thought, 'I will go over and see this strange sight – why the bush does not burn up.'

When the Lord saw that he had gone over to look, God called to him from within the bush, 'Moses, Moses!'

And Moses said, 'Here I am.'

'Do not come any closer,' God said. 'Take off your sandals, for the place where you are standing is holy ground.' Then he said, 'I am the God of your father, the God of Abraham, the God of Isaac and the God of Jacob.' At this, Moses hid his face, because he was afraid to look at God. . . .

God said to Moses, 'I am who I am. This is what you are to say to the Israelites: "I AM has sent me to you."' **(Exodus 3:1–6, 14)**

LEADER   This is from the Book of Job.

READER 1   A word was secretly brought to me, my ears
caught a whisper of it. Amid disquieting dreams
in the night, when deep sleep falls on men, fear
and trembling seized me and made all my bones
shake. A spirit glided past my face, and the hair
on my body stood on end. It stopped, but I could
not tell what it was. A form stood before my
eyes, and I heard a hushed voice.   **(Job 4:12–16)**

READER 2   Were a man to awaken in the pitch dark at midnight
and hear someone moving about in his room, and
know that the unseen presence was a loved member
of his family who had every right to be there, his
heart might be filled with a sense of quiet pleasure;
but should he have reason to believe that an intruder
had entered, perhaps to rob or to kill, he would lie in
terror and stare at the darkness not knowing from
which direction the expected blow might come. But
the difference between experience and no experience
would be that acute sense of someone there. Is it not
true that for most of us who call ourselves Christians
there is no real experience? We have substituted
theological ideas for an arresting encounter; we are
full of religious notions, but our great weakness is
that for our hearts there is no one there.*

[A. W. Tozer]

LEADER   Again, when a young man called Isaiah went to
worship, something happened to him which
completely altered his whole life:

READER 1   In the year that King Uzziah died, I saw the Lord
seated on a throne, high and exalted, and the
train of his robe filled the temple.
'Woe to me!' I cried. 'I am ruined! For I am a
man of unclean lips, and I live among a people of
unclean lips, and my eyes have seen the King,
the Lord Almighty.'   **(Isaiah 6:1, 5)**

LEADER   And Ezekiel, the prophet, experienced an awesome
vision in a prison camp and tried to describe it:

*From 'The Divine Conquest', A. W. Tozer, published Send the Light Trust

READER 2   This was the appearance of the likeness of the glory of the Lord. When I saw it, I fell face down, and I heard the voice of one speaking.

(Ezekiel 1:28b)

LEADER   In a similar way St John, on the prison colony island of Patmos, where he was one of a chain gang, said:

READER 1   When I saw him, I fell at his feet as though dead. Then he placed his right hand on me and said: 'Do not be afraid. I am the First and the Last. I am the Living One; I was dead, and behold I am alive for ever and ever! And I hold the keys of death and Hades.' **(Revelation 1:17–18)**

LEADER   Some experiences are uncanny and terrifying but the ones we are looking at today are awesome yet magnetic and somehow friendly. Listen again. This is the effect that Jesus of Nazareth had on so many:

READER 2   When he had finished speaking, he said to Simon, 'Put out into deep water, and let down the nets for a catch.'

Simon answered, 'Master, we've worked hard all night and haven't caught anything. But because you say so, I will let down the nets.'

When they had done so, they caught such a large number of fish that their nets began to break. So they signalled their partners in the other boat to come and help them, and they came and filled both boats so full that they began to sink.

When Simon Peter saw this, he fell at Jesus' knees and said, 'Go away from me, Lord; I am a sinful man!' **(Luke 5:4–8)**

LEADER   Hymn number 45/70/130

LEADER OR READER 1   Let us pray:

Mysterious Lord, whom we cannot see and whom we cannot find by searching or striving, help us today to be still and know you are God. Take away our feverish worries and nagging anxieties, our infernal busyness and grant us to be aware of your awesome majesty, your presence and your unchanging love. *Amen.*

The Lord's Prayer in more modern words:

Our Father in heaven, hallowed be your name, your kingdom come, your will be done on earth as it is in heaven. Give us today our daily bread. Forgive us our debts, as we also have forgiven our debtors. And lead us not into temptation, but deliver us from the evil one.　**(Matthew 6:9–13)**

For smaller gatherings

Preparation

1　Select the appropriate items from the foregoing presentation, adapt them where necessary and arrange with those taking part to be fully briefed.
2　Prepare your selection of readings and arrange for your readers to have copies of their texts and time to rehearse.

Additional ideas

If appropriate and useful in your opinion, introduce a sharing time when you invite the group to tell of any mysterious experience they have had. Be prepared, however, for contributions from them on:

(a)　The occult
　　Make it very plain that not only Christians but psychiatrists, psychologists and so many counsellors regard this as very dangerous. Even experimenting in this field can be the opening of a satanic Pandora's Box which they may not be able to close afterwards. Even apparently 'innocent games' which involve 'dark forces' produce horrific effects. Advise them that it is very dangerous to dabble in such 'games'.

(b)　Psychological experiences
　　'I've done all this before', or 'I've been here before' or 'I know what's coming next'.
　　Remember the rule: Never follow a complicated solution when a simple one is available.
　　Psychology and physics of the brain are so much more helpful than reincarnation theories, etc. For example, some experiences can be explained by errors of recognition caused by the similarity of two 'brain storage' patterns and by errors of function when the two hemispheres of the brain function with a split-second gap between them giving rise to a feeling of familiarity.

(c) Artificially induced states (drugs, drink, sniffing, etc.)
These are not the same experiences as 'the numinous'. They deaden and do not enliven a person. They lead to lower, not higher, awareness, they induce dependence not freedom, they need ever-increasing doses of stimulation and do lead to more rather than less dependence on any substance. They disintegrate the personality and do not integrate it and produce a loss rather than an increase of self-control.

Follow-up ideas

1 Arrange for a suitable doctor to come and answer questions from the group on the physical effects of drugs and alcohol, etc.
2 Arrange for a member of Alcoholics Anonymous to explain dependency and the difference and connection between
   (a) occasional social drinking,
   (b) regular heavy drinking, and
   (c) alcohol dependency.
3 If possible, arrange for a worker from a rehabilitation organisation to speak and answer questions.

9 Money, money, money

For larger assemblies

Leader's preparation

1   Read through the presentation and select those items you intend to use.
2   Look through the suggested material and if 'The £50 note' is to be used, decide whether it will be more effective in your assembly as a story, a mime or a play, and then prepare accordingly. This will involve careful rehearsals.
3   Collect examples of coins and notes, even some 'Monopoly' money and some foreign currency. Ask the school staff.
4   Arrange the readers, one for Scripture quotations and two for dialogues.
5   Arrange for taped or disc music and accompaniment to the hymns.
6   Select the prayer leader.

Assembly presentation

LEADER   Greetings!
(and fade in a tape of ABBA singing 'Money, money, money, it's a rich man's world' (CBS Records))
Today the theme of the assembly is money (fade out).

(STORY OR MIME)

LEADER   This is the story of a £50 note.

Once upon a time there was a lady who said to her husband, 'Keep this for me', and handed him a £50 note. The man put it in a cup on the shelf and both went out. Just then their boy came in. 'Mum,' he said, 'I need to borrow some money to pay for my motor bike repair . . . Oh, she's out. Hello, what's this?' He picked up the £50 note and said, 'I'll borrow this till tomorrow when I get paid.' He went and paid the mechanic who gave him a receipt and then put the £50 note in his pocket because he was just going out to lunch with three other men at the local pub.
  Each paid for his meal but the mechanic paid for the meal in full with the £50 note, receiving his

change and the money the others gave him for their
meals. The landlord of the pub put the note in the till
of the bar. A customer said, 'Your wife's coat is ready
and it looks good too.' 'How much?' asked the
landlord. 'Forty-nine pounds,' said the customer.

The landlord paid him with the £50 note. The
customer was a tailor who went back to his shop,
made up the wages, putting the £50 note in one
packet which was later given to one of the
employees, a boy who worked for him. The boy went
home, opened the packet and remembered he had
borrowed £50 from a cup on the shelf, so he replaced
it. His mother came in and said, 'Oh, thank
goodness, it's still there.' And tearing it up said, 'It
was a fake.' (Without any break instantly bring in
music for a few seconds and then begin to fade)

[Frank Cooke]

Money in itself is only bits of paper and metal. (Hold
up the examples, throwing the Monopoly money
away.) It is used as the symbol of goods and services.
What we are greedy for is what we think it will buy.
Listen now to the story of a young man who had
everything – well, he was very rich, he had power (he
was a ruler), he was young, and on top of all that, he
was a good-living man also. Yet even so he did not
feel he was really living. Something was missing.
Listen.

READER 1   As Jesus started on his way, a man ran up to him
and fell on his knees before him. 'Good teacher,'
he asked, 'what must I do to inherit eternal life?'

'Why do you call me good?' Jesus answered.
'No one is good – except God alone. You know
the commandments: "Do not murder, do not
commit adultery, do not steal, do not give false
testimony, do not defraud, honour your father
and mother."'

'Teacher,' he declared, 'all these I have kept
since I was a boy.'

Jesus looked at him and loved him. 'One thing
you lack,' he said. 'Go, sell everything you have
and give to the poor, and you will have treasure
in heaven. Then come, follow me.'

> At this the man's face fell. He went away sad,
> because he had great wealth.   **(Mark 10:17–22)**

LEADER   Jesus did *not* tell everyone to give away all their
money, but this man's money was stopping him from
really living. He had everything and was sick of it.

Hymn number 7/108

Now listen to this.

READER 2   'I must be the most miserable man on earth.'

READER 1   That was said by Jay Gould, the multi-millionaire.

READER 2   'For the *love* of money is a root of all kinds of evil.'
(I Timothy 6:10)

READER 1   The apostle Paul said that. Note he didn't say money
was the problem, but love of it.

READER 2   'You cannot serve both God and Money,'
(Matthew 6:24b)

READER 1   said Jesus.

READER 2   Marilyn Monroe, in her day, was the world's sex-
goddess, worshipped by millions of men, envied by
millions of girls. She ended by committing suicide,
heartbroken, wretched and alone.

READER 1   'What good is it for a man to gain the whole world,
yet forfeit his soul?'   **(Mark 8:36)**

READER 2   said Jesus.

LEADER   Now a prayer. Let us pray.

Lord, today we pray for those who are so poor that
they have nothing but money. We also pray for the
poor who have no money at all. Open our eyes to see
how important it is to share the necessities of life and
to see that it is our greed that destroys your world.
Amen.

READER 1   This is a story about St Philip Neri who lived between
1515 and 1595. It is called 'St Philip and the student'.

READER 2   One day St Philip Neri was talking with a young
student of the university, whose worldly prospects
were very flattering, and whose ambition was great.

St Philip asked him what was to be his career.

'I am now studying philosophy,' he replied, 'but I shall finish my philosophical course next year.'

'And then?' asked St Philip.

'Why, then I shall study the full course of canon and civil law, and take my cap as a doctor.'

'And then?' asked St Philip again.

'Then I shall practise as an advocate, and make for myself a reputation.'

'And then?' asked the saint once more.

'Then I shall marry, and succeed to the estates of my family, and become an auditor of the rota, and perhaps rise still higher.'

'And then?' still asked St Philip.

'Why, then I suppose I shall be satisfied with the position I have won, and shall be respected by my fellow-citizens; and, like everybody else, shall grow old, and die.'

'And then?' St Philip still enquired.

The young man hesitated; his lips quivered. His ambitious dream had been dispelled by the two simple words.*

LEADER And now a prayer. Let us pray.

Lord, you do not judge by what we give but by what we keep for ourselves. Put a generous spirit within us so that we share what we truly value with those who need it.

Since you said that it is more blessed to give than to receive, help us to discover the joy of giving thoughtfully and systematically, our money, our time, our attention and our friendship to those we meet and work with and those we live with day by day. *Amen.*

Hymn number 58/109

---

*From 'Lectionary of Christian Prose' compiled A. C. Bouquet, published Longman Green and Co. Ltd.

For smaller gatherings

Preparation

Select the appropriate items from the foregoing presentation, adapt them where necessary and arrange with those taking part to be fully briefed.

Additional ideas

The following Bible quiz is suitable only for smaller gatherings. The quiz should be copied out so as to provide every child with a version on which to write his/her answers. A Bible should also be available to each child. The 'answers' are provided for the Leader only so that by exchanging papers the children may mark each other's answers and as they do so discuss the questions raised. Adapt it to suit your group.

BIBLE QUIZ
Write down answers numbered 1–10

1   What happened to the rich farmer Jesus described who spent his life in hoarding?
2   Does the Bible say:
    'Money is the root of all evil?'   Yes/No
3   Fill in the missing word:
    'You cannot serve both God and _____.'
4   Why did Jesus say, 'But woe to you who are rich'?
5   How many things are we told not to covet by the tenth commandment? Try and write down as many as you can.
6   Why should we not be anxious about what we shall eat or drink or wear?
7   In Deuteronomy 8 what are the chief dangers in having everything we need?
8   'A man's life does not consist in the abundance of his _____.' Fill in the missing word.
9   Fill in the missing words: 'But when you give to the needy, do not let your left hand know _____.'
10 What do the words of the last question mean?

ANSWERS
  1 See Luke 12:16–21.
  2 No. See I Timothy 6:10.
  3 Money. See Luke 16:13.
  4 'For you have already received your comfort.' Luke 6:24.
  5 Seven. See Exodus 20:17. Put some of these into a modern equivalent, for example ox = car; donkey = station wagon.
  6 Because your heavenly Father knows you need them all. See Matthew 6:31–33.
  7 See Deuteronomy 8:12–14, 17–18.
  8 Possessions. See Luke 12:15.
  9 'What your right hand is doing.' See Matthew 6:3.
 10 Give secretly and not for the reward of the applause of friends. Matthew 6:4.

Follow-up idea

Read twice or have read by two members of the group the following poem:

                    If I had a million pounds

   I would buy me a perfect island home,
   Sweet set in a southern sea,
   And there would I build me a paradise
   For the heart o' my Love and me.

   I would plant me a perfect garden there,
   The one that my dream soul knows,
   And the years would flow as the petals grow,
   That flame to a perfect rose.

   I would build me a perfect temple there,
   A shrine where my Christ might dwell,
   And then would I wake to behold my soul
   Damned deep in a perfect hell.
                         [G. A. Studdert Kennedy]

Then
(a) Ask your group what they think the poet had in mind.
(b) Lead them in a discussion on the trap of trying to buy one's way out of life's duties and privileges.
(c) Ask why the poet thought that Christ would not dwell in such a temple.

10 Strength of character

For larger assemblies

Leader's preparation

1 Read through the presentation and select those items you intend to use.
2 Arrange for the two readers to have the text of their script and time to be rehearsed.
3 Arrange for the musical accompaniment for the hymns.
4 Enlist a senior pupil to lead the prayers and prepare for that by pondering the prayers printed here or by writing his/her own.

Assembly presentation

LEADER   Greetings!
C. S. Lewis wrote a book called *The Screwtape Letters* which pretended to be letters from a senior devil to a junior tempter on how to destroy a human being by temptation. Here is a bit of one of the letters:

READER 1   My dear Wormwood,
So! Your man is in love – and in the worst kind he could possibly have fallen into – and with a girl who does not even appear in the report you sent me.
I have looked up the girl's dossier and am horrified at what I find. Not only a Christian but such a Christian – a vile, sneaking, simpering, demure, monosyllabic, mouse-like, watery, insignificant, virginal, bread-and-butter miss. The little brute. She makes me vomit. She stinks and scalds through the very pages of the dossier. It drives me mad, the way the world has worsened. We'd have had her to the arena in the old days. That's what her sort is made for. Not that she'd do much good there, either. A two-faced little cheat (I know the sort) who looks as if she'd faint at the sight of blood and then dies with a smile. Why doesn't the Enemy blast her

for it, if he's so moonstruck by virginity – instead of looking on there, grinning? [Remember that by 'the Enemy' he means God]

He has filled his world full of pleasures. There are things for humans to do all day long without his minding in the least – sleeping, washing, eating, drinking, making love, playing, praying, working. Everything has to be twisted before it's any use to us. We fight under cruel disadvantages.

LEADER   The devil cannot create, he can only take God's good gifts and corrupt them. God the creator tells us how his gifts, his world and we ourselves work.

READER 2   The Ten Commandments:

I am the Lord your God, who brought you out of Egypt, out of the land of slavery.
You shall have no other gods before me.

READER 2   You shall not make for yourself an idol in the form of anything in heaven above or on the earth beneath or in the waters below. You shall not bow down to them or worship them; for I, the Lord your God, am a jealous God, punishing the children for the sin of the fathers to the third and fourth generation of those who hate me, but showing love to thousands who love me and keep my commandments.

READER 1   You shall not misuse the name of the Lord your God, for the Lord will not hold anyone guiltless who misuses his name.

READER 2   Remember the Sabbath day by keeping it holy. Six days you shall labour and do all your work, but the seventh day is a Sabbath to the Lord your God. On it you shall not do any work, neither you, nor your son or daughter, nor your manservant or maidservant, nor your animals, nor the alien within your gates. For in six days the Lord made the heavens and the earth, the sea, and all that is in them, but he rested on the seventh day. Therefore the Lord blessed the Sabbath day and made it holy.

READER 1   Honour your father and your mother, so that you may live long in the land the Lord your God is giving you.

READER 2   You shall not murder.

READER 1   You shall not commit adultery.

READER 2   You shall not steal.

READER 1   You shall not give false testimony against your neighbour.

READER 2   You shall not covet your neighbour's house. You shall not covet your neighbour's wife, or his manservant or maidservant, his ox or donkey, or anything that belongs to your neighbour.

(Exodus 20:2–17)

LEADER   Hymn number 23/26/10

LEADER   During the Second World War Nazi concentration camps were extermination factories. Millions of Jews and political prisoners were executed. Those camps were like hell on earth. Here is what a survivor of one of those camps wrote.

READER 1   All I know is that when it became hardest of all for men to behave like decent human beings they spread their wings and rose to great heights; and when the strains and temptations were removed, they sank into the mud.
   In their heart of hearts they may have felt, as I did, that in its way, it was the life of the camp that was the true life, the life that bore witness to what really counted in humanity, the spirit . . . . This for me is the first lesson of the camp, that it made beasts of some men, saints of others, and the second lesson is that it is hard to predict who will be the saint and who the beast when the time of trial comes. Only one thing prevailed – strength of character. Cleverness, creativeness, learning, all went down: only real goodness survived.*   [Pierre d'Harcourt]

*From 'The Real Enemy' by Pierre d'Harcourt, published Longman Group Ltd.

LEADER   Your strength of character is what you really are under pressure.

In the book *Lord Jim* by Joseph Conrad, the hero, an educated Englishman, second in command of a merchant ship, was panicked by a treacherous crew into abandoning ship in a storm believing it to be sinking. Eight hundred helpless passengers, pilgrims to Mecca, were left to drown, but the ship did not sink, and there were hundreds of witnesses to his cowardice. He spent his life trying to live down the moment when at the time of testing he panicked and ran. His character was stained.

A SENIOR PUPIL   Let us pray:

Lord, have mercy upon us and forgive our cowardice and weakness when we are under pressure,
the lust we call love,
the loudness we call courage,
the flattery we call tact,
the laziness we call leisure,
the prejudice we call opinion and
the greed we call need.
Lord, put the steel of self-discipline into our souls that we be not controlled by our animal nature but inspired by the strength, humility and love of Jesus. *Amen*.

If you know it, join with me in saying the Lord's Prayer:

Our Father, which art in heaven, Hallowed be thy name. Thy kingdom come. Thy will be done in earth, as it is in heaven. Give us this day our daily bread. And forgive us our debts, as we forgive our debtors.
And lead us not into temptation, but deliver us from evil:
For thine is the kingdom, and the power, and the glory, for ever. *Amen*.

LEADER   Hymn number 75/8

For smaller gatherings

Preparation

1 Select the appropriate items from the foregoing presentation, adapt them where necessary and arrange with those taking part to be fully briefed.
2 Arrange a day or more ahead for a sharing time by announcing that you intend to ask for one-sentence confessions of 'things that really do scare me to death'.

    The aim is to discover and discuss some of the panic points and try to find out why they are there (see 2 below).

Additional ideas

1 If the teacher is familiar with George Orwell's *1984* he can explain and then discuss the interrogation methods of the 'thought police'. They broke down resisting characters by taking them over their personal panic threshold.
2 In the 'panic level' discussion try, by the use of any training in psychology and by common sense to help the children to face their fears and realise that everyone has fears and panic thresholds. Courage is not being unafraid but overcoming fear. You may wish to invite a trained counsellor to share in such a session.
3 An extra quotation:

> Strong men are not always 'tough guys'.
> In the making of a legend, the normal pattern is that the hero becomes more and more heroic and more removed from ordinary mortals by his remarkable powers, but not this man. From a carpenter's shop he is portrayed as one vulnerable to all human need, loving children and flowers, fearlessly talking about God and man in the most earthy and controversial terms, painting vivid word pictures of the 'kingdom of heaven' and holding a mirror to the human race as no other being had done before him or since. He knew what it was to be hungry and thirsty. He could laugh and weep. He could speak with such gripping power that the listening crowd even forgot about eating! Yet when he was on trial for his life, he refused to defend himself and remained silent. When men expected him to be proud and to stand on his dignity, he took the task of the lowest slave and washed the dirty feet of his guests. When they expected him to be humble, he made claims which sounded outrageous enough to be labelled

'blasphemous'. He made friends of social rejects, he stayed in the homes of outcasts, courageously faced the combined weight of the might of the Roman state, orthodox religion and the chanting of a fickle mob. Yet his sensitive mind shrank from the violence of torture and death which he so clearly saw approaching. This is no wild-eyed fanatic. He did not die in glorious martyrdom. This is not the raw material of super-heroes. This is the record of a man whose personality and behaviour could not be pigeon-holed in our man-sized boxes, even by those very writers themselves. To this day there strides out of the New Testament pages the man who splits history in two. This is the man whose name millions of men use daily as a curse and millions of others revere as God.

This is Jesus.

[Frank Cooke]

Follow-up idea

Using the group's own admitted and listed fears begin an ongoing project in which they are encouraged to help younger children by each selecting and befriending one child who is timid or shy or vulnerable or handicapped and occasionally to 'report back' on their own feelings as they progress. Do not permit open discussion or naming of any other children.

11 Why praise God?

For larger assemblies

Leader's preparation

1   Read through the presentation and select those items you intend to use.
2   If you wish to use the suggested teaching aid using the seven letters in the word 'worship', it will require more preparation than simply chalking the letters on a board or cutting them out and attaching them to a wall display. Each letter and its word needs more filling out than has been given in the text.

Freedom is allowed for personal interpretation and particular application, for example:

Word	should explain the significance of such Old and New Testament lessons. Verses helpful in preparation: Luke 4:16–21 (see pages 69).
Offering	The money given should be a real offering and not loose change. Explain why. God judges us not by what we give but by what we keep for ourselves. Verses helpful in preparation: Luke 21:1–4 (see page 69).
Reverence	includes behaviour and attitudes and thinking magnificently about God. Verse helpful in preparation: John 4:23 (see page 70).
Spirit	Worship in the Spirit means knowing that God is present and that worship is supernatural as well as natural. Verse helpful in preparation: John 4:23 (see page 70).
Hymns	Unselfconscious singing is a great liberator and full of enjoyment. Verses helpful in preparation: Psalm 95:1–2 (see page 70).
Instruction	If there is a positive and inspiring Bible teacher in the area, go and learn – it's dynamite! Verses helpful in preparation: Matthew 28:19–20 (see page 70).
Prayer	Team prayer is much more than saying prayers. It is a power line.

Verses helpful in preparation: Philippians 4:6–7 (see page 71).

3 Arrange for the two readers and give them opportunity to rehearse.

4 Arrange for the musical accompaniment of the hymns and if possible a recording of inspiring church music to play before and after the assembly, for example:

   (a) 'The Arrival of the Queen of Sheba' from *Solomon* by G. F. Handel,

   (b) Toccata and Fugue in D minor by J. S. Bach,

   (c) 'The Old Hundredth' as sung to the hymn 'All people that on earth do dwell' (BBC recording of the Coronation of Her Majesty Queen Elizabeth II).

5 If you have a Hebrew-speaking person in school, enlist him or her to teach the school how to say the best-known Hebrew words such as:

Hallelujah	Praise the Lord
Amen	So be it
Messiah	The anointed (king) or in Greek 'Ho Christos' (The Christ).

6 If overhead projection is available it might be possible to show slides of various worship occasions. These would need to be collected privately and could include views of:

   St Peter's Square in Rome at Easter,
   The Oberammergau Passion Play,
   Bethlehem at Christmas,
   A Billy Graham rally in a football stadium, etc.

Assembly presentation

LEADER Greetings!
This morning I ask why all this emphasis in almost every religion about praising God? C. S. Lewis was a Christian scholar who was simply brilliant at explaining the Christian faith in simple terms, yet he said:

READER 1 When I first drew near to belief in God . . . I found it a stumbling-block that 'we should praise God'. Still more, that God himself demanded it!

LEADER We all despise those people who have to be fawned on and flattered and constantly praised. Surely God isn't the supreme egotist having to be told by all heaven and earth that he is great and marvellous and wonderful? Lewis discovered just the opposite was the truth. Only God is selfless enough to be able to be praised without it making him swollen-headed or conceited. So, we praise God, not for what it does to *him* but what it does to *us*. Lewis went on:

READER 2   But the most obvious fact about praise – whether of God or anything – strangely escaped me. I thought of it in terms of compliment, approval, or the giving of honour. I had never noticed that all enjoyment spontaneously overflows into praise unless (sometimes even if) shyness or the fear of boring others is deliberately brought in to check it. The world rings with praise – lovers praising their mistresses, readers their favourite poet, walkers praising the countryside, players praising their favourite game – praise of weather, wines, dishes, actors, motors, horses, colleges, countries, historical personages, children, flowers, mountains, rare stamps, rare beetles, even sometimes politicians or scholars. I had not noticed how the humblest, and at the same time most balanced and capacious, minds, praised most, while the cranks, misfits and malcontents praised least. I had not noticed either that just as men spontaneously praise whatever they value, so they spontaneously urge us to join them in praising it: 'Isn't she lovely? Wasn't it glorious? Don't you think that magnificent?' I think we delight to praise what we enjoy because the praise not merely expresses but completes the enjoyment.*

LEADER   That is why praising God is so important. I mean really enjoying him as the one we value most. He is worth more than everything else: Worth-ship, in fact is the root of the word worship. Now that's worth singing about!

Let us praise God as we sing hymn number 6/30/15

LEADER   Let's see if we can find a simple way of remembering some of the things which make real worship a living thing.
    Here are some letters: let's see what they stand for. (Visual aid to be adapted and developed as the leader wishes. See leader's preparation 2.)

*From 'Reflections on the Psalms' by C. S. Lewis, published Fontana

W is for Word

All religions rely on a written word. For Jews the Old Testament is the book to study, for Christians the Old and New Testaments are their written authority. Christians believe that the key to open the Bible is Jesus. Being a Jew he not only accepted the Old Testament's authority but he revealed its eternal foundations, fulfilled its promises and obeyed its moral commands. Listen to his first sermon in his own home town of Nazareth:

READER 1   He went to Nazareth, where he had been brought up, and on the Sabbath day he went into the synagogue, as was his custom. And he stood up to read. The scroll of the prophet Isaiah was handed to him. Unrolling it, he found the place where it is written: 'The Spirit of the Lord is on me, because he has anointed me to preach good news to the poor. He has sent me to proclaim freedom for the prisoners and recovery of sight for the blind, to release the oppressed, to proclaim the year of the Lord's favour.'

Then he rolled up the scroll, gave it back to the attendant and sat down. The eyes of everyone in the synagogue were fastened on him, and he said to them, 'Today this scripture is fulfilled in your hearing.'   **(Luke 4:16–21)**

LEADER   *O is for Offering*

In worship the giving of money is not a collection; that's what you do in a coach by passing round the hat for the driver. An offering of money means the giving of ourselves to God who gives himself to us freely. God does not judge what we give but what we keep for ourselves. What we give says, 'I love you this much, Lord'.

READER 2   As he looked up, Jesus saw the rich putting their gifts into the temple treasury. He also saw a poor widow put in two very small copper coins. 'I tell you the truth,' he said, 'this poor widow has put in more than all the others. All these people gave their gifts out of their wealth; but she out of her poverty put in all she had to live on.'   **(Luke 21:1–4)**

LEADER   *R is for Reality and Reverence*
If worship isn't real, it's another R – rigmarole. It becomes real when we put ourselves and our soiled little lives before the only absolutely true, absolutely pure, absolutely good, loving and all-seeing being of the universe. Don't get too pally with Almighty God.

LEADER   *S stands for Spirit and Supernatural*
God does not look on what we say or do so much as why and how and what we are. The Holy Spirit is God moving inside people who invite him into their lives. Then worship really comes alive and is both natural and supernatural. Jesus gave only two main guidelines for worship and we have just glanced at them both. In the Bible truth means what is genuine – real. Listen:

READER 1   Yet a time is coming and has now come when the true worshippers will worship the Father in spirit and truth, for they are the kind of worshippers the Father seeks.   **(John 4:23)**

LEADER   *H stands for Hymns*
Unselfconscious singing can be a great liberator. We sing at football matches. We sing at birthday parties, even if only 'Happy birthday to you', we sing in all kinds of celebration, and we sing in worship. Listen:

READER 2   Come, let us sing for joy to the Lord, let us shout aloud to the Rock of our salvation. Let us come before him with thanksgiving and extol him with music and song.   **(Psalm 95:1–2)**

LEADER   *I stands for Instruction*
All true worship is an educator; it teaches people how to pray by praying. They learn to praise by praising and they learn the great themes of the Bible by hearing and doing. Listen to this:

READER 1   Jesus said, 'Therefore go and make disciples of all nations, baptising them in the name of the Father and of the Son and of the Holy Spirit, and teaching them to obey everything I have commanded you. And surely I will be with you always, to the very end of the age.'   **(Matthew 28:19–20)**

LEADER   *P stands for Prayer*
In worship we pray together as a team. Prayer is
much more than saying our prayers; it is a way of
listening to God and replying to him, when we mean
what we say and say what we mean. In it we can give
thanks to God, ask for things he wants to give us,
pray for others and even apologise to him for what
we have done wrong and listen to his reply.

READER 2   Do not be anxious about anything, but in
everything, by prayer and petition, with
thanksgiving, present your requests to God. And
the peace of God, which transcends all
understanding, will guard your hearts and your
minds in Christ Jesus.   **(Philippians 4:6–7)**

LEADER   Put the seven letters together and they spell
WORSHIP, the highest activity humans can manage.
Let us say together the Lord's Prayer (see page 168.)
Let us sing hymn number 41/49
(If slides are available and ready project them during
a Psalm of praise.)

READER 1   Sing to the Lord a new song; sing to the Lord, all
the earth. Sing to the Lord, praise his name;
proclaim his salvation day after day. Declare his
glory among the nations, his marvellous deeds
among all peoples.
   For great is the Lord and most worthy of
praise; he is to be feared above all gods. For all
the gods of the nations are idols, but the Lord
made the heavens. Splendour and majesty are
before him; strength and glory are in his
sanctuary.
   Ascribe to the Lord, O families of nations,
ascribe to the Lord glory and strength. Ascribe to
the Lord the glory due to his name; bring an
offering and come into his courts. Worship the
Lord in the splendour of his holiness; tremble
before him, all the earth.
   Say among the nations, 'The Lord reigns.' The
world is firmly established, it cannot be moved;
he will judge the peoples with equity.
   Let the heavens rejoice, let the earth be glad;
let the sea resound, and all that is in it; let the

fields be jubilant, and everything in them. Then
all the trees of the forest will sing for joy; they
will sing before the Lord, for he comes, he comes
to judge the earth. He will judge the world in
righteousness and all the peoples in his truth.

(Psalm 96)

LEADER   There are two words from the ancient Hebrew
language which everyone, all over the world, knows.
One is 'Hallelujah' which means 'Praise the Lord' and
the other is 'Amen' which means 'so be it – we agree'.
Let's hear you all speak Hebrew and say in that
language 'Praise the Lord' – and now 'Let's all agree'.
Another is the Hebrew title for the king, the
anointed. It is 'Messiah' or if you want it in Greek it is
'Ho Christos', the Christ!

True worship is the highest activity human nature
is capable of performing. Listen to some of the things
it involves:

READER 2   'To worship God is
to quicken the conscience by the holiness of God,
to feed the mind with the truth of God,
to purge the imagination with the beauty of God,
to open the heart to the love of God,
to devote the will to the purposes of God.'

[William Temple]

LEADER   Someone once said that today's world is like a shop
window where all the price tags have been switched
around and some cheap little object is valued at
thousands of pounds while a priceless treasure is
marked at a few pence.

True worship is where we put all the labels back in
the right places.

READER 1   'To come aside from the world's half truth, lying and
lust, its money-grubbing, power-crazed, bitter,
argumentative swamp and stand in the presence of
the only one absolutely true, pure, loving, wise and
good person is surely the most necessary thing a man
can do, even if he only does that once a week.'

LEADER   When a woman asked Jesus where and how you
worship he said simply this:

READER 2 'Believe me, woman, a time is coming when you will worship the Father neither on this mountain nor in Jerusalem.' **(John 4:21)**

LEADER So the master pattern of worship is a rhythm of God giving himself to us and our responding to him, and the only guidelines Jesus gave were these two things: that it should be in the Spirit of God and real!

Hymn number 71/91

For smaller gatherings

Preparation

Select the appropriate items from the foregoing presentation, adapt them where necessary and arrange with those taking part to be fully briefed.

If you do use the visual aid make sure you have planned it well.

Additional ideas

1 Arrange weeks ahead of this session for teams of say three pupils to visit services of worship in churches of different persuasions and even places of worship of different religions. Report back at a 'findings' session. You might invite ministers to answer questions.
2 Attempt a worship project. Together encourage the group to create a meaningful Act of Worship in which the whole school could share. To do this
    (a) Request permission from both the head and the group to lead the whole assembly at an agreed date.
    (b) Let the group suggest the various ingredients of the Act of Worship, and arrange them in good order.
    (c) Arrange for the music, decide who should take part and have a full rehearsal.
    (d) Use all the 'gifts' of the group in word, song, movement and music.

Follow-up idea

Arrange for a special showing of 'Visions', a video film of dance, music and drama (2 hours) from Religious and Moral Education Press.

12   Faith

For larger assemblies

Leader's preparation

1   Read through the presentation and select those items you intend to use.
2   If you decide to use the sketch
    (a)   Choose two characters from among those scholars who have a gift for this sort of thing.
    (b)   Let them have copies of the script in enough time for them to learn their lines and rehearse them until they flow naturally. They could keep their lines with them as 'prompt sheets'.
    (c)   Rehearse with them and arrange for them to 'enter' and 'exit' in the shortest possible time.
3   Select the cast and rehearse the 'wedding'. This can be done without being ponderous, and although it is bound to be a giggly subject it can be handled seriously but with a light touch so that the points will stick despite some embarrassment about the subject. The point can be made by simply reading the vows, but this will be less effective than enacting them.
4   Arrange for the musical accompaniment for the hymns.
5   If you wish to use the acted parable decide if you wish to demonstrate it yourself or have two people act it. If you do it yourself use a willing student or even a pillow (if you wish to clown a little). If you involve two characters, choose them. One could be a member of staff as the doctor; give them their lines and rehearse with them until they flow naturally.
    The only 'props' required are an extra table and cushion for the patient to lie on for the examination.
    Instruct the 'actors' to look at each other as they speak and when you speak to them to look at you until the assembly is over.

Assembly presentation

LEADER   Greetings!
             This morning we start with hymn number 129/9

LEADER   Now following that, listen to this poem by Emily Dickinson:

READER   I never saw a moor,
I never saw the sea;
Yet know I how the heather looks,
And what a wave must be.

I never spoke with God,
Nor visited in heaven;
Yet certain am I of the spot
As if the chart were given.

LEADER   So that lady who lived well over a hundred years ago set out in two little verses the argument that you can know some things for sure even though you have not seen them. Seeing is not believing but believing is seeing.

Let's eavesdrop on this scene in a school somewhere in Britain.

SKETCH

SPEAKER A   I need proof, I tell you. All this faith business is make-believe. It's like Father Christmas and the tooth fairy.

SPEAKER B   No, it's not like that. I've never watched a nuclear explosion, seen my brains or been in a coal-pit, but I know what they are like and I know they are real.

SPEAKER A   Don't be stupid. Everyone knows about things like that.

SPEAKER B   How?

SPEAKER A   Because millions of people who have seen them have told us . . . . We even have photographs, TV programmes, and all that. In short, mate, evidence!

SPEAKER B   So you accept the evidence of reliable witnesses?

SPEAKER A   Of course I do. Our law courts depend on the evidence of eye-witnesses.

SPEAKER B   And so do I. Millions of people who have experienced and known God can't all be wrong and they are witnesses to what they have experienced themselves.

SPEAKER A   I need more proof.

SPEAKER B   What kind of proof would you accept?

SPEAKER A You know, scientific proof, like litmus paper changing colour.

SPEAKER B That's fine for acids and alkalis but you can't test that your Mum loves you by dipping her into a glass.

SPEAKER A No, that's different.

SPEAKER B Of course it is. Everything worth knowing is tested in a different way, and in the end, it isn't just God that you know by faith. You can't know anything without faith.

SPEAKER A What's that, you can't know anything . . .

SPEAKER B That's right . . .

(They exit still arguing)

LEADER Thank you. Now listen to this reading, because Jews, Muslims and Christians all honour Abraham as the father of real faith.

READER By faith Abraham, when called to go to a place he would later receive as his inheritance, obeyed and went, even though he did not know where he was going. By faith he made his home in the promised land like a stranger in a foreign country; he lived in tents, as did Isaac and Jacob, who were heirs with him of the same promise. For he was looking forward to the city with foundations, whose architect and builder is God.

(Hebrews 11:8–10)

LEADER Hymn number 90/89

LEADER Faith is not blind belief. It is an attitude of trust in another person or persons, so it is a part, the deepest part, of a relationship. Let's re-enact the best known act of faith in this country. We call it a wedding, for whether it is in church or in a registry office, certain words must be said. It is the law of the land.

I have enlisted some help from two of our students who know that they run the risk of your pulling their legs about this but they are brave enough to do it, just the same.

(Enter students and a member of staff. They take

up their places facing off stage so that all three faces can be seen.)

MINISTER OR
REGISTRAR
I do solemnly declare (pause while Charlie repeats) that I know not of any lawful impediment why I (repeat), Charlie Brown (repeat), may not be married to Mary Smith (repeat).

(All this repeated, the names reversed and this time Mary speaking.)

Charlie, will you have Mary to be your lawful wife? Will you love her, comfort her, honour and keep her, in sickness and in health for as long as you both shall live?

CHARLIE I will.

(Same words repeated to Mary.)

MARY I will.

LEADER It gets even more specific and demanding as they take each other's hand and continue:

CHARLIE I call upon these persons here present to witness that I, Charlie, do take you, Mary, to be my lawful wife, from this day forward, for better, for worse, for richer, for poorer, in sickness and in health, to love and to cherish till death do us part.

(Mary then repeats, the names reversed.)

LEADER Thank you. You have been very brave.
(The trio exit quickly or sit down on stage.)
Don't worry. They have not really been married but think of what they said and we even left out the giving and receiving of a ring!
It would be unthinkable for them to pick and choose: 'Can I take her for health only', 'Can I take him for richer and not poorer', because they are making a commitment to each other presumably because they love each other. Neither knows what tomorrow will bring but in faith they promise their lives to each other – that is an act of faith.
This is what all great religions of the world mean by faith in God. The Christian faith means putting one's trust in Jesus as Saviour and Lord and God and this is

worked out in a living relationship with God like in a good marriage where the couple love each other and trust each other.

And now a prayer.

Today, Lord, we pray for the gift of faith in you which trusts when it cannot feel and walks with you even in the darkest valleys, knowing for sure that 'Even though I walk through the valley of the shadow of death, I will fear no evil, for you are with me.' Thank you, Lord, that I can trust you, especially as I cannot trust myself. *Amen.*

Thought for today: Jesus said, 'Have faith in God.'

(Mark 11:22)

And now an acted parable. (See leader's preparation 5: Doctor seats himself at the table.)

DOCTOR   'Next please' (enter student).
'Sit down. Now what seems to be the trouble?'

PATIENT   'I've got this sharp pain in my tummy.'

DOCTOR   'How long have you had it?'

PATIENT   'Two days now and it's getting worse.'

DOCTOR   'Lie down on the table. I'll examine you.'
(The patient lies down and the doctor takes the pulse and temperature and begins to press on the tummy. Suddenly the patient shouts:)

PATIENT   'Ow! That hurt.'

DOCTOR   'Just there?' (and presses again)

PATIENT   (very loud) 'Yes, there!' (sits up)

DOCTOR   'You've got appendicitis, that's all. All you have to do is come into the clinic right away and I'll operate on you.

PATIENT   'Not on me, you won't!'

DOCTOR   'Why, don't you believe me?'

PATIENT   'Yes, of course I believe you. You're the doctor.'

DOCTOR   'Well then . . .?'

PATIENT   'You're not cutting me open.'

DOCTOR	'Don't you trust me?'
PATIENT	'Well . . . er . . .'
LEADER	(interrupting: doctor and patient sit down, looking at the leader) 'Yes, he believes you but does not trust you! He believes what you say but he has no faith in you. Is that right?' (turning to the patient)
PATIENT	'That's right, I suppose.'
LEADER	So it's possible to believe and still die because you haven't got faith. Let's leave it there.

For smaller gatherings

Preparation

1 Select the appropriate items from the foregoing presentation, adapt them where necessary and arrange with those taking part to be fully briefed.
2 Whichever sketch you use, afterwards encourage a 'sharing time' (not an argument or even a discussion) on living faith in the experience of the group members. Simply let those with anything to say, speak.
3 In the sharing distinguish between
   (a) *practical* everyday *faith* (i.e., every time we get on a bus, a train or a plane we put our trust in those responsible for the driving and signalling, flying and maintaining efficiency). Let the group jointly compile a list of some of the major examples of everyday faith we all need and start off the list with the pre-operative injection before being taken into an operating theatre when the patient puts himself totally into the doctor's hands;
   (b) the *'saving faith'* of the New Testament, i.e. total trust in Jesus as Saviour and Lord.

Follow-up idea

'Looking at Faith' is a 40 mm video film about different faiths prepared for children from 8 to 11 years of age which could easily be adapted for your group. Notes for teacher and pupils are provided. It is available from Religious and Moral Education Press.

13 Hidden people-shapers!

For larger assemblies

Leader's preparation

1 Read through the presentation and select those items you intend to use.
2 Arrange for the readers (three or four) and see that they have a copy of their texts and time to rehearse their lines.
3 Have a record or tape of a small part of the Beatles' 'All you need is love' (Polydor/EMI records).
4 Assemble from private transparencies for overhead projector picture examples of, say, a little girl hugging a kitten; someone nursing a baby; a fireman carrying someone from a burning building; a bride and groom on their wedding day – any pictures expressing devotion, care, commitment. An enquiry and request from the staff alone should produce dozens of transparencies and you only require a few.
5 Arrange for the musical accompaniment for the hymns.

Assembly presentation

LEADER   Greetings!
Today I am going to read you an outline of a case study described by Dr Margaret Ribble.

Little Bob was born in the maternity hospital in New York and he weighed 6lb 3oz. For two weeks everything was normal, his mother feeding him and the baby thriving. On reaching home his mother found that her husband had deserted her. She was so angry and shocked that it affected her milk, and the baby, who began vomiting and refusing her milk, was taken into hospital and abandoned there. In spite of skilled feeding and careful attention the baby gained no weight, and at the age of two months weighed 5lb. After four months he looked like a seven-month foetus, his arms and legs wrinkled and wasted, his head out of proportion, his skin cold and flabby. He took large quantities of milk but gained no weight. He sweated severely, especially during sleep and was gradually wasting away. A nurse was assigned to 'mother' him, to carry him about, talk to him, and of course feed him from the bottle. He began to improve slowly and was taken to a foster home. He was slow to develop though his IQ was high, but any change in his routine sent him into a deep depression, for his emotional life was severely damaged.

Bob may never be capable of loving and may always be an emotional cripple, never realising that his problems all stem from being rejected or simply not being loved when he needed it.*

We are shaped by things hidden from us.

READER 1   A school bully may not realise that inside he is terrified of not being noticed. 'Please look at me and admire me,' he is really saying.

READER 2   A grossly overweight person may eat as a love- or mother-substitute, and deep down is saying, 'Please love me. I need to be full of love.'

READER 1   The school lover, for ever boasting of sexual exploits, may well be crying out for attention, secretly saying, 'Don't ignore me. See how admirable I am!' He is really so insecure that without admiration he shrivels up.

LEADER   All these, and many others, boil down to something so important that without it every human being grows up warped and starved within. That something is described here as the greatest thing in the world.

READER 2   If I speak in the tongues of men and of angels, but have not love, I am only a resounding gong or a clanging cymbal. If I have the gift of prophecy and can fathom all mysteries and all knowledge, and if I have a faith that can remove mountains, but have not love, I am nothing. If I give all I possess to the poor and surrender my body to the flames, but have not love, I gain nothing.

Love is patient, love is kind. It does not envy, it does not boast, it is not proud. It is not rude, it

*Quoted from 'The Root of the Matter' by Margaret Isherwood, published Harper Ltd.

is not self-seeking, it is not easily angered, it
keeps no record of wrongs. Love does not
delight in evil but rejoices with the truth. It
always protects, always trusts, always hopes,
always perseveres.
  Love never fails . . . .
  And now these three remain: faith, hope and
love. But the greatest of these is love.

(I Corinthians 13:1–8a, 13)

LEADER   Well, if it's that great, is it this?
(Fade in the first part of the Beatles' record 'All you
need is love'. Run for a short time and fade as you
talk over and show slides.)
  Yes, love is the greatest thing in the world but is it
this? or this? or this?
(Show a number of pictures – see leader's
preparation. If it is too difficult to do the visual
display describe a little girl hugging a kitten, a mother
nursing her baby, a fireman carrying someone from a
burning building, a bride and groom on their
wedding day, a crucifix – compile your own display.)
  Yes, it *is* these and much, much more. Let's sing
about it now.

Hymn number 79/128

CHORAL READING
(three voices)

RABBIT   'What is REAL?'

NARRATOR   asked the rabbit one day, when they were lying side
by side near the nursery fender, before Nana came to
tidy the room.

RABBIT   'Does it mean having things that buzz inside you and
a stick-out handle?'

SKIN HORSE   'Real isn't how you are made,'

NARRATOR   said the skin horse.

SKIN HORSE   'It's a thing that happens to you. When a child loves
you for a long, long time, not just to play with, but
REALLY loves you, then you become Real.'

RABBIT 'Does it happen all at once, like being wound up, or bit by bit?'

SKIN HORSE 'It doesn't happen all at once,'

NARRATOR said the skin horse.

SKIN HORSE 'You become. It takes a long time. That's why it doesn't often happen to people who break easily, or have sharp edges, or who have to be carefully kept. Generally, by the time you are Real, most of your hair has been loved off, and your eyes drop out and you get loose in the joints and very shabby.'

[M. Williams Biance]

LEADER The best-known verse in the Bible is

'For God so loved the world that he gave his one and only Son, that whoever believes in him shall not perish but have eternal life.' **(John 3:16)**

And now a prayer.

Help us, Lord, to love by knowing that you love us more than anyone else in the world does, by putting the feelings of others before our own selfish feelings, and by doing what we know is right rather than what we feel like doing. Help us here today in school to show love by doing the best we can in everything and by being strong enough to be truly kind to each other. Make us sensitive to those who are lonely, unhappy, picked on or bullied, laughed at or scorned, made fun of because of the way they look or speak, and make us brave enough to befriend them and stand with them. *Amen*.

On a lighter note, how about this sarcastic poem published anonymously by the *Daily Telegraph*, which demonstrates the way millions are shaped by red tape?

O thou who seest all things below
Grant that thy servants may go slow,
That they may study to comply
With regulations 'til they die.

Teach us, O Lord, to reverence
Committees more than common sense;
To train our minds to make no plan
And pass the baby when we can.

So when the tempter seeks to give
Us feelings of initiative
Or when alone we go too far,
Chastise us with a circular.

'Mid war and tumult, fire and storms,
Give strength, O Lord, to deal out forms;
Thus may thy servants ever be
A flock of perfect sheep for thee!

There's nothing like a vast bureaucracy to brainwash
and shape people by pouring them into a mould, so
be on your guard: don't be shaped against your better
judgement. Refuse to do things merely because
everyone else does them or simply to impress the
people you want to accept you. It takes real courage
to be yourself and real humility to admit you did
something just to impress the others.

And now a hymn. 140/139

For smaller gatherings

Preparation

1 Select the appropriate items from the foregoing presentation, adapt
   them where necessary and arrange with those taking part to be
   briefed.
2 Pre-arrange for the group to bring in their favourite records or tapes
   to play a sample passage and say why they like it. Encourage an open
   discussion on each example.

Additional ideas

1   Let the group chalk up ten of the most important items of today's smartest fashion styles in hair, dress, footwear, ornaments and status symbols, and open a discussion on 'Why we think these are smart'. The aim is to show how 'shaped' we are by 'what everyone else does'. Keep pressing behind the explanation to show that the bottom line is to impress the people we want to like and accept us.

2   If you have experience in a psychological approach draw out your group's daydreams and dreams of glory, and without humiliating anyone underline the real desire for fame and personal adulation.

3   See follow-up idea below.

4   See also 'Forbidden fruit' and 'The story of two camels' (in Extra Material).

Follow-up idea

Depending upon the enthusiasm of your group, develop a wall montage to which they may add, as their grasp grows of the people-shapers, cartoons, photographs and magazine pictures of Hitler Youth, emotional pop concerts, gang fights, 'smart young things' and children's styles of the 1890s and every decade to the present, including punks, pop stars, cowboys and cops.

The unspoken aim is to see on a wide backcloth the generation-shapers, under the heading 'The things that shape us'.

14   Courage and fear

For larger assemblies

Leader's preparation

1 Read through the presentation and select those items you intend to use.
2 Prepare the three readers; give them copies of their scripts and time to rehearse.
3 Arrange for the musical accompaniment for the hymns.
4 If you decide to include the interviews or testimony, take care not to overdo the bravery congratulation.

   Choose an interviewer from the staff or senior school, to be briefed as follows: The interviewer should meet well beforehand those he is to interview, get to know their stories and mannerisms well and compile a list of questions, which should not overrun the time allowed. Opening and closing sentences should be prepared. Every school has pupils who have shown courage in the face of danger or adversity. From these select one or two willing to be interviewed about their

   (a) harrowing hospital treatment,
   (b) terrifying ordeal in a natural calamity,
   (c) fight to overcome mental or physical handicap,
   (d) experience in an accident, fire or other emergency,
   (e) being trapped without panicking, etc. etc.

   Ensure that the interview is matter-of-fact and does not even hint at producing admiration for or flattery of the subject, but an objective report such as a good TV interview might be. Arrange the seating, amplification and a smooth entrance and exit procedure for the interviewer and those interviewed.

Assembly presentation

LEADER   Greetings!
Have you ever been in the house alone and started to get nervous? Suddenly you hear all kinds of noises you hadn't noticed before – the creaking of furniture, water pipes expanding or contracting, thermostats cutting in and out. Then you start thinking 'Perhaps I'm not alone in here'. Once you start thinking that

your heart starts thumping and you are wide awake listening to the roaring silence, every nerve jangling. You would swear that you can hear someone breathing, then the stairs creak. If a cat squawked at that moment you'd jump out of your skin! Now, you may not ever admit to being afraid, but real bravery is never found in those who do not feel fear. It can only be found in people who do know what it is to be afraid. Courage is the power of mind to overcome fear.

That is our theme today: courage.

Let us sing.

Hymn number 94/38

LEADER   People who are not afraid of anything should scare us to death! If they are telling the truth they are human freaks. It is more likely that they are so terrified of being called cowards that they will do anything to escape that reputation. So it's fear and not courage that drives them after all. They make themselves big because they are afraid of being small.

Listen to the words of a young man who knew he had done nothing 'wrong and yet was about to be arrested, tortured, flayed and then nailed up through his wrists and ankles with 10-inch spikes on to a huge cross. He was no fanatic, unafraid of death – he shrank from it, but he overcame his fear.

READER 1   They went to a place called Gethsemane, and Jesus said to his disciples, 'Sit here while I pray.' He took Peter, James and John along with him, and he began to be deeply distressed and troubled. 'My soul is overwhelmed with sorrow to the point of death,' he said to them. 'Stay here and keep watch.'

Going a little farther, he fell to the ground and prayed that if possible the hour might pass from him. 'Abba, Father,' he said, 'everything is possible for you. Take this cup from me. Yet not what I will, but what you will.'

Then he returned to his disciples and found them sleeping. 'Simon,' he said to Peter, 'are you asleep? Could you not keep watch for one hour? Watch and pray so that you will not fall into temptation. The spirit is willing, but the body is weak.'

Once more he went away and prayed the same thing. When he came back, he again found them sleeping, because their eyes were heavy. They did not know what to say to him.

Returning the third time, he said to them, 'Are you still sleeping and resting? Enough! The hour has come. Look, the Son of Man is betrayed into the hands of sinners. Rise! Let us go! Here comes my betrayer!'   **(Mark 14:32–42)**

LEADER   Let us pray.

Lord, strengthen us by the Holy Spirit so that when we are afraid of being ridiculed for doing what is right, when we are mocked because of our size or shape or colour, when we are afraid of owning up to the truth of our wrongdoing, when we are in danger and see others in danger and can help, give us the power to overcome fear and do what we know is right.

Deliver us from the cowardice which blames everyone except ourselves, freezes in the face of danger and when hurt, blindly lashes out to escape the pain of humiliation. Lord, give us the courage of Jesus, we pray, courage to stand by those who are victimised, courage to stand up for what is true, and courage to stand even if all others turn and run from the truth. *Amen*.

Let's be daring now and put someone's courage to the test. If I were to invite any sincere believer in God to come up here now and explain to us all why he or she believes in God – I did not say to come and say why you do not believe because it is too easy to curry popularity by being negative: I said, if you do believe, come up now and say why you do believe. That will be a real contribution to our assembly and a demonstration of how fear can be overcome. Right here, right now!

(Anything or nothing can happen at this point! Do not be afraid of waiting a little.)

The Greek word for witness is *martyr* and a Christian lawyer called Tertullian is believed to have been the reporter of the martyrdom of St Perpetua about AD 200. Listen.

READER 2   Two young Christian women were brought in, one a delicate young girl called Perpetua and the other Felicity, fresh from childbirth. They were stripped, wrapped up in nets and gored by a wild bull. Perpetua was tossed first and fell on her hip. She sat up and asked for a hairpin to fix her dishevelled hair. She went to help Felicity who had been gored and she helped her stand. A leopard had been turned loose on a young Christian man called Saturninus who was soon bathed in his own blood. They were all finally brought to the middle of the arena to be finished off with the sword, Perpetua guiding the hand of the young gladiator to pierce her throat.

LEADER   So died thousands of Christian martyrs who, rather than disown Jesus their Lord, embraced most brutal torture and death with shining faith and unblemished courage. It makes us realise how quickly we give way to fear.

Hymn number 101/42

LEADER   And now I would like to introduce . . . who for the next few moments is our interviewer.

INTERVIEWER   Hello, and let me introduce to you . . . who, as you may know, has been through quite an ordeal lately. (One or two short interviews to follow.)

LEADER   Thank you.
Not every brave person is publicly acknowledged and not every coward is publicly disgraced. The same raw material out of which cowardice and courage are made is in every one of us. It is called *fear*.

We will close with hymn number 33/114/144

For smaller gatherings

Preparation

1 Select the appropriate items from the foregoing presentation, adapt them where necessary and arrange with those taking part to be fully briefed.
2 The items suggested in the presentation will, as ever, require some adaptation but should be more effective in a smaller and more informal setting.

Additional ideas

Develop and adapt the item in the presentation for large assemblies in which everyone in the groups is challenged to stand up, come forward and tell the group something which he/she has found to be real and worthwhile.

Follow-up idea

Plan for a future gathering by enlisting volunteers who agree to write short scripts or essays to be read aloud by them (or by others) on the subject 'The bravest person I've met' or 'The bravest person I've read about' – they should explain why they think these people are brave. These essays should be brought to a planning and briefing session at a time and on an agreed date and the chosen pieces would form the bulk of some future assembly which would be linked together like beads on a necklace by the leader's comments and observations.

15   Serves you right!

For larger assemblies

Leader's preparation

1   Read through the presentation and select those items you intend to use.
2   Arrange two readers and provide them with a copy of the scripts and time for them to rehearse.
     If you decide to use the two readers for the prayers mark their scripts and in rehearsing them insist they pause after each petition to let it sink in.
3   Arrange the musical accompaniment to the hymns and any solos or duets suggested by the music staff.
4   If possible, plan ahead and prepare a display of cause and effect in human behaviour, for example,
     (a) posters of children playing with matches;
     (b) posters of kettles of boiling water within reach of children (from the British Safety Council);
     (c) posters about smoking and the link with lung cancer (from the Health Education Council or ASH);
     (d) publicity regarding the effect of drugs (also Health Education Council);
     (e) publicity about promiscuous sexual intercourse; government leaflet on AIDS;
     (f) anything else you would want to publicise, plus leaflets from all these agencies.
The display should be well set out, described at the assembly and given a prominent place in the school for one week.

Assembly presentation

LEADER   Greetings!
Today we start with a hymn.

Hymn number 111/127

LEADER   In a hospital ward in one of our big cities a young man lay partly paralysed following a horrific accident involving his motorbike and a car. Everyone felt so sorry for him and, what was worse, he even felt sorry for himself.

READER 1
(a boy)

He would say each day, 'Why me, what have I done to deserve this? I'll never walk again, never play football, never make love. I might as well be dead. Why me?'

READER 2
(a girl)

A young nurse who really cared about him said to him one day, 'Look, you chose this when you chose to show off, going at 100 mph and deliberately taking risks to look macho. You chose this.' And she added: 'We love you enough to do anything in our power to help, but don't sow your wild oats and pray for a bad harvest.'

LEADER
(repeats)

'Don't sow your wild oats and pray for a bad harvest.' In this world we are responsible for what we choose to do and life does send in its bills:

'Sow a thought, reap a deed;
Sow a deed, reap a habit;
Sow a habit, reap a character;
Sow a character, reap a destiny.'

Our theme today is our responsibility for what we become.

LEADER OR
READERS 1
AND 2
alternately

Lord, give us the grace to accept the responsibility for our decisions and to make no excuse when we reap what we sow (* = pause).

When we sow aggression and arrogance and reap hatred,*
When we sow laziness and idleness and fail to qualify in anything,*
When we sow lust and are consumed by its fire and are left with cold ashes,*
When we seek release by drugs and stimuli knowing that we will become enslaved by our dependency,*
When we seek popularity and the approval of our friends at any price and thus become puppets allowing *them* to pull the strings,*
When we sow lawlessness and therefore become criminals,*
When we sow violence thinking we can disown the harvest of mutilation and murder,*
When we sow cruelty and become stone-hardened and brutish,*
Instead, give us courage to do and to be what we

know is right and build a life on firm foundations, that sowing goodness we may reap, if we faint not, a harvest of joy, through Jesus Christ our Lord. *Amen*.

READER 1   Do not be deceived: God cannot be mocked. A man reaps what he sows.   **(Galatians 6:7)**

(An additional lesson if required)

READER 2   You, my brothers, were called to be free. But do not use your freedom to indulge the sinful nature; rather, serve one another in love. The entire law is summed up in a single command, 'Love your neighbour as yourself.' If you keep on biting and devouring each other, watch out or you will be destroyed by each other. So I say, live by the Spirit, and you will not gratify the desires of the sinful nature. For the sinful nature desires what is contrary to the Spirit, and the Spirit what is contrary to the sinful nature. They are in conflict with each other, so that you do not do what you want. But if you are led by the Spirit, you are not under law.
The acts of the sinful nature are obvious: sexual immorality, impurity and debauchery; idolatry and witchcraft; hatred, discord, jealousy, fits of rage, selfish ambition, dissensions, factions and envy; drunkenness, orgies, and the like. I warn you, as I did before, that those who live like this will not inherit the kingdom of God.
         (Galatians 5:13–21)

LEADER   Hymn number 62/20

LEADER   'It serves you right' can be quite an accurate statement. It can be used as a terrible weapon by callous, loveless people. In other words, for us to say it to ourselves is right; for us to say it to someone else is almost always wrong.
    So, let's apply it to ourselves – 'It serves me right!'

READER 1   When I steal, because whether I'm caught or not, I have become a thief,

READER 2   When I lie, whether I am found out or not, I am a liar,

READER 1   When I lose control, whatever the reason, I am being destroyed,

READER 2　When I laugh, speak or listen, I am revealing my personality and the way it is being shaped.

LEADER　We often regret it when the result of our action comes home to us.

　　Now remember. We can be sorry for what we've done but that does not necessarily put everything right. I can be sorry I spilt ink on the tablecloth, but my regret doesn't wash out the stain.

　　I can be sorry I stole something but my sorrow does not put the thing back.

　　I can be sorry I didn't wear a crash helmet but regret does not mend my broken skull.

　　A real change comes about when we are sorry enough to quit whatever we are doing and if possible put things right. Sometimes just to face our own responsibility is our great need.

　　Listen to a searching poem by Sydney Carter:

READER 1　You who are 17
blame me because
the world is in a mess.

When I was seventeen
we talked about
the Treaty of Versailles.

And so we pass
the buck right back to Adam;
so let me

Ask, in the name of
my small son,
aged 3,

About insecticide,
the colour bar,
the H bomb,
and the pill.

You will be 31
when he is 17.
What (if anything)

Will you have done
to dodge the accusation
of my son?

LEADER   A doctor reported that when people come to him with signs and symptoms of venereal disease, many try to evade responsibility saying that they must have caught it from a toilet seat or a cracked cup. Even when he has said, 'No, you get it from having sexual intercourse with an infected person', the usual response of the patient is to curse and blame someone for giving it to him. He went on to say, 'It never seems to occur to them that *they chose this* by being promiscuous. Every time they have random sex they are at risk. They accepted the risk and they lost.'

For smaller gatherings

Preparation

1   Select the appropriate items from the foregoing presentation, adapt them where necessary and arrange with those taking part to be fully briefed.
2   If you decide to use the additional suggestion, a good local video film shop would be able to furnish catalogues.

Additional ideas

1   The TV companies have many excellent 25-minute videos on most of the addictive social habits and their effects on families. There are also video films of the 'consequences' of other anti-social activities. The occasional use of such films followed by brief discussions on them can be informative and helpful.
2   See also 'Well?' (in Extra material).

Follow-up idea

Begin a compassion diary and in it list those who 'did not get away with it' and are now left with the terrible consequences brought upon themselves. Start a list and keep adding to it categories of people whom you will pray for regularly in future assemblies and find out from the relevant agencies if any other help could be given. The list could begin for example with:

  prisoners serving sentences for crime, drug addicts trying to break the dependency, gamblers and alcoholics.

16   True grit

For larger assemblies

Explanation. In this unit there is an overlap with the item on 'Courage and fear' on page 86. The focal point is somewhat different here; determination and grit is examined rather than courage.

Leader's preparation

1   Read through the presentation and select those items you intend to use.
2   If possible, arrange an interview or brief address, five minutes or so, featuring someone perhaps living locally who has overcome great difficulties such as loss of limbs, sight or hearing, and who by determination and perseverance has triumphed. If this suggestion is adopted follow the preparations as set out in the unit 'Courage and fear' on page 86.
3   Arrange for three readers to have copies of the text and opportunity for rehearsal.
4   Arrange for the musical accompaniment for the hymn.
    If you choose to include the musical item the school's music leader should be approached well ahead and asked if a solo, duet, group or choir could be rehearsed and presented.
    It could be one of the following hymns: 44/137/9/113

Assembly presentation

LEADER   Greetings!
          He was 19 years of age and had been brought up never to drink alcohol. The first time he went out drinking he got hopelessly drunk, took a short cut home, fell down a railway embankment and a goods train severed both his legs below the knee. Throughout his recovery period and learning to walk on artificial legs he felt no bitterness, for as he said, 'No one else was to blame. It was all my own fault.'
          Despite his artificial legs he did a two-day rock-climbing course in his native Cornwall and

decided that he was going to be a mountaineer. He soon discovered that mountaineering takes more training and fitness than rock-climbing and his trainer advised a toughening-up course. So in 1969 he walked the 900 miles from John o' Groats to Land's End. It took him three months overcoming the agony of the artificial limbs splitting and blistering his stumps. He persevered and climbed in the Alps, Peru, Argentina, Kashmir and China, climbing mountains of over 20,000 ft.

In 1976 he was the star of BBC's 'This is your Life' and received the OBE in 1977. He raises money for charities by his mountaineering. He is called Norman Croucher and his book *A Man and his Mountains* illustrates how sheer determination can conquer mountains.

Now listen to this:

READER 1   Are they Hebrews? So am I. Are they Israelites? So am I. Are they Abraham's descendants? So am I. Are they servants of Christ? (I am out of my mind to talk like this.) I am more. I have worked much harder, been in prison more frequently, been flogged more severely, and been exposed to death again and again. Five times I received from the Jews the forty lashes minus one. Three times I was beaten with rods, once I was stoned, three times I was shipwrecked, I spent a night and a day in the open sea. I have been constantly on the move. I have been in danger from rivers, in danger from bandits, in danger from my own countrymen, in danger from Gentiles; in danger in the city, in danger in the country, in danger at sea; and in danger from false brothers. I have laboured and toiled and have often gone without sleep; I have known hunger and thirst and have often gone without food; I have been cold and naked. Besides everything else, I face daily the pressure of my concern for all the churches.   **(II Corinthians 11:22–28)**

LEADER (Interview/guest spot. See leader's preparation 2.)
Thanks to our guest.

Hymn number 52/4/64

READER 1 Let us pray.

A prayer of thanksgiving.
Thank you, Lord, for giving us the inspiration of
courageous, persevering souls who in spite of great
hardship and handicaps have battled through and
prevailed. Thank you for those whose perseverance
has given us our language, our heritage, our
industries, our medicine, anaesthetics and surgery,
our mines, agriculture, music, poetry, theatre, radio
and TV. For all the myriads of blessings which have
come to us through the determination of others we
give you, Lord, our grateful thanks. Through Jesus
Christ our Lord. *Amen.*

LEADER Here is a quotation from the diary of John Wesley:

READER 2 In the evening, as I was preaching at St Ives, Satan
began to fight for his kingdom. The mob of the town
burst into the room and created much disturbance;
roaring and striking those that stood in the way, as
though Legion himself possessed them. I would fain
have persuaded our people to stand still; but the zeal
of some and the fear of others, had no ears; so that
finding the uproar increase I went into the midst and
brought the head of the mob up with me to the desk.
I received but one blow on the side of the ear: after
which we reasoned the case, till he grew milder and
milder, and at length undertook to quiet his
companions.*

LEADER John Wesley was a man who travelled constantly,
worked ceaselessly, by iron self-discipline lived
frugally; never lost his temper or his zeal for Jesus.
He was a man whose true grit was a true gift of the
Holy Spirit.
Now here is a musical item (solo, duet, group or
choir).

*From 'Lectionary of Christian Prose' compiled A. C. Bouquet, published Longman Green and Co.
Ltd.

LEADER	Years ago, statistics were compiled by an American insurance company about the prospects of a hundred keen men, all 25 years old, starting out in business. At 65 those men would have fallen into the following classes:
READER 3	36 would be dead, 54 would be financially dependent, 5 would be barely able to pay their way, 4 would be comfortably off, 1 would be rich.*
LEADER	Insurance companies make allowances for many who begin well but end poorly. Our concern is the defect in human character which for most people means not having the power to see things through. There is all the difference in the world between being a good starter and a good finisher. Let's ask some questions which don't require answers:
READER 1	Every day, how many people begin to slim but give it up?
READER 2	How many people today will give up smoking but not keep it up?
READER 1	How many people today will begin trying to play a musical instrument?
READER 2	There is a very large market in almost new second-hand guitars!
READER 1	How many people setting out on a car journey today won't arrive?
READER 2	How many students today will complete the workload they themselves have chosen to do?
LEADER	So many millions of people, as Jesus said, 'begin to build, but are not able to finish'. The power to see it through is what we are calling true grit. It does not come by accident but is, according to the Bible, a gift of God – 'steadfast endurance'.

*From 'Twelve Tests of Character' by H. E. Fosdick, published Association Press Ltd.

You might run a mile race and lead the field throughout but if you fall 10 yards from the finish that is what will be remembered.

So let our final prayer be for the power to see it through.

READER 3 Lord, we do not know what problems we will encounter as we get older. We do not know what others will do to us, nor whether we will be sick or well, rich or poor, but we ask you now for the gift of true grit which overcomes self-pity, self-excuse and self-satisfaction and goes on to the end, until it completes the course you have set us. *Amen.*

For smaller gatherings

Preparation

1 Select the appropriate items from the foregoing presentation, adapt them where necessary and arrange with those taking part to be fully briefed.
2 If you wish to use the additional idea decide how best to present it to your group but not for discussion, rather as an end piece.

Additional idea

Here is the story of a humble woman:

I was living at Sandy Hook when I met Jacob Walker. He kept the Sandy Hook lighthouse. He took me to that lighthouse as his bride. I enjoyed that, for it was on land, and I could keep a garden and raise vegetables and flowers.

After a few years my husband was transferred to Robbins Reef. The day we came here I said: 'I won't stay. The sight of water whichever way I look makes me lonesome and blue.' I refused to unpack my trunks and boxes at first. I unpacked them a little at a time. After a while they were all unpacked and I stayed on . . . .

My husband caught a heavy cold while tending the light. It turned into pneumonia. It was necessary to take him to the Smith Infirmary on Staten Island, where he could have better care than I could give him in the lighthouse.

I could not leave the light to be with him. He understood. One night, while I sat up there tending the light, I saw a boat coming. Something told me what news it was bringing me. I expected the words that came up to me from the darkness.

'We are sorry, Mrs Walker, but your husband's worse.'

'He is dead,' I said.

We buried him in the cemetery on the hill. Every morning when the sun comes up I stand at the porthole and look in the direction of his grave. . . . Sometimes the hills are white with snow. Sometimes they are green. Sometimes brown. But there always seems to come a message from that grave. It is what I heard Jacob say more often than anything else in his life. Just three words: 'Mind that light.'

Mrs Walker, still keeping the light, was seventy years old when the reporter interviewed her, and her husband had been dead thirty-two years.*

Follow-up idea

It might be a useful exercise over a period of say four months to challenge your group to compile a list of true stories of true grit and human endurance from classic biographies, The Reader's Digest, paperbacks, magazines, etc. and at an agreed date those stories could be presented in abbreviated form to the group by those who had read them and had been impressed by them.

*From 'Twelve Tests of Character' by H. E. Fosdick, published Association Press Ltd.

17   Christmas is coming

For larger assemblies

Leader's preparation

1   Read through the presentation and select those items you intend to use.
2   Begin with up-to-date news about any Christmas celebration or events at school.
3   Arrange for the two readers to have copies of their lines and opportunity to be rehearsed.
4   Arrange for the musical accompaniment for the assembly carols and for any group or ensemble which might take part today with special music.
5   Arrange for them to rehearse their item and also for their entry and exit to be as silent and speedy as possible.

Assembly presentation

LEADER   Greetings!
It will soon be Christmas and today's theme is about getting ready for Christmas. We will begin with a carol.

Hymn number 74/55

LEADER   Now let the late John Betjeman set the scene for us:

READER 1   'Christmas'

The bells of waiting Advent ring,
    The Tortoise stove is lit again
And lamp-oil light across the night
    Has caught the streaks of winter rain
In many a stained-glass window sheen
From Crimson Lake to Hooker's Green.

The holly in the windy hedge
    And round the Manor House the yew
Will soon be stripped to deck the ledge,
    The altar, font and arch and pew,
So that the villagers can say
'The church looks nice' on Christmas Day.

Provincial public houses blaze
   And Corporation tramcars clang,
On lighted tenements I gaze
   Where paper decorations hang,
And bunting in the red Town Hall
Says 'Merry Christmas to you all'.

All London shops on Christmas Eve
   Are strung with silver bells and flowers
As hurrying clerks the City leave
   To pigeon-haunted classic towers,
And marbled clouds go scudding by
The many-steepled London sky.

And girls in slacks remember Dad,
   And oafish louts remember Mum,
And sleepless children's hearts are glad,
   And Christmas-morning bells say 'Come!'
Even to shining ones who dwell
Safe in the Dorchester Hotel.

LEADER   But the poem goes on

READER 1   And is it true? And is it true,
   This most tremendous tale of all,
Seen in a stained-glass window's hue,
   A Baby in an ox's stall?
The Maker of the stars and sea
Become a Child on earth for me?

LEADER   Is it true, this most tremendous tale of all? Here is one of the accounts of the story in the New Testament.

READER 2   In those days Caesar Augustus issued a decree that a census should be taken of the entire Roman world. (This was the first census that took place while Quirinius was governor of Syria.) And everyone went to his own town to register.
    So Joseph also went up from the town of Nazareth in Galilee to Judea, to Bethlehem the town of David, because he belonged to the house and line of David. He went there to register with Mary, who was pledged to be married to him and was expecting a child. While they were there, the time came for the baby to be born, and

she gave birth to her firstborn, a son. She
wrapped him in strips of cloth and placed him in
a manger, because there was no room for them in
the inn.

And there were shepherds living out in the
fields near by, keeping watch over their flocks at
night. An angel of the Lord appeared to them,
and the glory of the Lord shone around them,
and they were terrified. But the angel said to
them, 'Do not be afraid. I bring you good news of
great joy that will be for all the people. Today in
the town of David a Saviour has been born to
you; he is Christ the Lord. This will be a sign to
you: You will find a baby wrapped in strips of
cloth and lying in a manger.'   **(Luke 2:1–12)**

LEADER   Hymn number 13/40/11/142

READER 1   And is it true? For if it is,
    No loving fingers tying strings
Around those tissued fripperies,
    The sweet and silly Christmas things,
Bath salts and inexpensive scent
And hideous tie so kindly meant,

No love that in a family dwells,
    No carolling in frosty air,
Nor all the steeple-shaking bells
    Can with this single Truth compare –
That God was Man in Palestine
And lives today in Bread and Wine.

LEADER   That last line worries some Christians because the
real point of the poem is the Christmas message 'that
God was Man in Palestine'. The living being of God is
much more than any bread and any wine!

Let us pray.

Lord, who as at this time entered fully into our world
that we might enter fully into yours, grant us truly to
see you and in seeing you to love you and in loving
you to grow more like you, this very day. *Amen.*

READER 2   They all were looking for a king
To slay their foes and lift them high:

Thou cam'st, a little baby thing
That made a woman cry.

[George Macdonald]

LEADER And now a carol. Hymn number 126/122/106

LEADER What *is* the meaning of this festival? Let us hear one of Dr W. E. Sangster's stories from a Christmas sermon he preached:

READER 1 Dr Stanley Jones has told a story of a little boy who stood before a picture of his absent father, and then turned to his mother and said wistfully: 'I wish Father would step out of the picture.'

That little boy expressed, in his own way, the deepest hope of the deepest souls who lived before Christ. They believed in God! Socrates and Plato did – the finest of the Greeks. The ancient Eastern sages did: Gautama, the Buddha; Lao-tze, the Chinese teacher; Akhnaton, the most profoundly religious of the Pharoahs. With overpowering intensity the Hebrew prophets did: Isaiah, Jeremiah, Ezekiel, and all the rest of them.

They believed in God! They believed that God could be seen in nature. He had made the world. In many ways, it was a picture of him. Indeed the most daring of them rose even to believe that the great Creator of the universe might be called a Father. They got as high as that – but farther than that they could not go. 'I wish that Father would step out of the picture.' Oh, for a warm heart in the universe! If only the Father would step out of the picture . . . .

Listen! Listen!

He *stepped* out of the picture. He stepped out at Bethlehem. Here is the glorious truth of it: 'The Word became flesh and dwelt among us . . . . No man hath seen God at any time; the only-begotten Son, which is in the bosom of the Father, he hath declared him.'

LEADER And now some special music for Christmas:

READER 2 Light looked down and beheld Darkness.
'Thither will I go,' said Light.
Peace looked down and beheld War.
'Thither will I go,' said Peace.

Love looked down and beheld Hatred.
'Thither will I go,' said Love.
So came Light and shone.
So came Peace and gave rest.
So came Love and brought Life.

[L. Housman]

LEADER   Let us pray.

Invisible yet ever-present God whom we see so
perfectly in the humanity and person of Jesus, we
marvel at the mystery of
    the unknowable who comes to be known,
    the all-powerful who puts himself at human mercy,
    the ever-present limited to one place and time,
    the majesty of eternity in a cowshed,
    the unimaginable power nailed to a cross,
    the eternal wisdom rejected and spat on by fools.
For your love in coming, your grace in self-giving and
your mercy in forgiving we praise and adore your
holy name. Through the same Jesus Christ our Lord.
Amen.

For smaller gatherings

Preparation

1   Select the appropriate items from the foregoing presentation, adapt
them where necessary and arrange with those taking part to be fully
briefed.

2   Open a discussion on 'What would make Christmas truly happy for
various people with problems. What could we do to help, if
anything?'

3   Are there people to whom we need to write 'Thank you' letters to
enclose with our cards? Allow five minutes for a list to be prepared
and ten to share it as a group, giving reasons.

4   Have some ideas and suggestions ready if you decide to attempt the
additional suggestion (1). For example, check with the local authority
and the local DHSS for suitable old people's homes and the name and
telephone number of the warden.

5   If you decide to attempt the follow-up suggestion, first contact the
children's officer at the local Social Services Department. Then if your

group is enthusiastic about helping and doing the work, begin to plan with them a brief carol-singing visit.

6   If you decide to do your own version of one of these it might be helpful to contact also local church ministers, Rotary Club and Round Table, as well as social workers, in order to discover the real needs and where those needs are.

Additional ideas

1   Discuss with the group what they might do to make Christmas a little happier for some elderly people in sheltered housing in the school vicinity in the form of a mini-carol concert. Have the various tasks all written out on cards and let them fill in the day and the time in order to explain to their parents.

2   If your group has the musical ability, leadership and the will to arrange and rehearse a small carol-singing group with guitar accompaniment (and any other suitable instruments such as flutes and recorders), then arrange for them to visit and sing to one or even two local old people's homes at a day and time agreed with the warden. Time could be taken in the assembly to arrange for a programme of carols, readings and a greeting to be given. What is agreed should be carefully noted for your reference.

3   See 'An eye for an eye' (Extra material)

4   See 'The bird that talked' (Page 151 'Is anyone there?')

Follow-up idea

In almost every community the local authority children's officer and staff know of needy children in the area. If the group is enthusiastic to plan it properly (with your help) and carry it out, a new or almost-new toy collection could be started, packaged and at an agreed time delivered. Any of your children not able to contribute toys could be urged to prepare letters and cards to enclose in the parcels.

18 Christmas (almost) present

For larger assemblies

Leader's preparation

1 Read through the presentation and select those items you intend to use.
2 Arrange for the musical accompaniment of the carols and, if possible and desirable, a singing group or choir to lead the singing and open the assembly with an introit.
3 Choose and rehearse two readers and possibly one other to lead the prayers.
4 If there is a school Christmas tree, that might be a good place to begin today's assembly, especially if the children are bringing gifts to be given to the under-privileged in the area.

Assembly presentation

(Music group/choir/or solo begin by singing (unannounced?) hymn number 37/67/105/121

LEADER Greetings!
Today's theme centres on the giving of presents in our celebration of Christmas.

Why do we give presents? The answer is provided in one of the New Testament's accounts of the birth of Jesus.

READER 1 After Jesus was born in Bethlehem in Judea, during the time of King Herod, Magi from the east came to Jerusalem and asked, 'Where is the one who has been born king of the Jews? We saw his star in the east and have come to worship him,' . . .

After they had heard the king (*telling them to search for the young child*), they went on their way, and the star they had seen in the east went ahead of them until it stopped over the place where the child was. When they saw the star, they were overjoyed. On coming to the house, they saw the child with his mother Mary, and they bowed down and worshipped him. Then they opened their treasures and presented him with gifts of gold and of incense and of myrrh. And having been warned in a dream not to go back to Herod, they returned to their country by another route. **(Matthew 2:1–2, 9–12)**

LEADER So they presented their gifts: gold, a gift for a king, incense, a gift for a priest, and myrrh, a gift to someone dead or dying, as if to say that here was a king who was also priest and a sacrifice all in one.

This is why some of the Christmas carols speak of this.

Take notice of the words as we all sing hymn number 134

LEADER Instead of asking you what you are *getting* for Christmas, I am asking you to consider what you are *giving* this Christmas, because real giving always means something more than the gift. Listen.

READER 2 One Christmas Santa Claus brought me a toy engine. I took it with me to the convent and played with it while mother and the old nuns discussed old times. But it was a young nun who brought us in to see the crib. When I saw the Holy Child in the manger I was very distressed because, little as I had, he had nothing at all. For me it was fresh proof of the incompetence of Santa Claus. I asked the young nun politely if the Holy Child didn't like toys, and she replied composedly enough: 'Oh, he does, but his mother is too poor to afford them.' That settled it. My mother was poor too, but at Christmas she at least managed to buy me something, even if it was only a box of crayons. I distinctly remember getting into the crib and putting the engine between his outstretched arms. I probably showed him how to wind it as well, because a small baby like that would not be clever enough to know. I remember too the tearful feeling of reckless generosity with which I left him there in the nightly darkness of the chapel, clutching my toy engine to his chest.   [Frank O' Connor]

LEADER Let us pray.
(or READER 3)

Lord Jesus, you were born into a poor family – we thank you for our families.

People brought you gifts which told what you had come to do – let our giving also be real and express thoughtfulness.

You came into a crowded town packed with busy people; we pray today for the busy people who are shopping, driving, governing, making, delivering, protecting, typing, computing, loving and caring, laughing and crying. Lord, let there be room for Jesus amid all this busyness.

You came to give heavenly gifts and you also accepted small human gifts and used them. Accept the gift of our lives to you this day and use them for the joy of others, we humbly pray. *Amen.*

READER 1   The Legend of the Other Wise Man by Henry van Dyke tells the story of Artaban, a Median from the city of Ecbatana. Along with the wise men, Caspar, Melchior and Balthazar, he also recognised from the heavens and ancient writings that a longed-for king, worthy of worship, was to be born King of Israel. He sold all his possessions and purchased a sapphire, a ruby and a pearl to carry them to give to the new king. He set out on his journey but did not arrive in time to meet his companions at the Temple of the Seven Spheres. He stopped to save the life of a poor man who was dying and arrived to find the message to follow them across the desert.

To do this he had to sell his sapphire to buy food and camels and he arrived at Bethlehem so late that the child king he sought had been taken to Egypt, and fierce soldiers came from the power-jealous King Herod to murder all the little boys of two and under.

He saved a child's life by bribing a soldier with the ruby and he was sad that he now had only one gift left for the king.

Artaban sought his king for years and did not find him, and his journey brought him at Passover to the city of Jerusalem, which seemed to be in uproar. 'We are going to Golgotha outside the walls to see two robbers crucified and a young man called Jesus who said he was king of the Jews.' This was surely the king he had sought for thirty-three years. He went with the crowds. When he was almost there a girl in great distress fell at his feet, pleading for help. She was to be sold as a slave for her father's debts. He gave her the one gift he still had, the pearl, as her ransom.

Just then in the strange darkness which had fallen in the afternoon, an earthquake rocked the city and they crouched in terror. A roof slate fell on Artaban and now he was dying and had failed to give his gifts to the king. But as he lay there he looked up and said with puzzled wonder radiating from his face – 'But when did I see you hungry and fed you . . . sick or in prison and came to you? Three and thirty years I have looked for you but have never seen your face nor ministered to you' – and the rescued maid heard a voice saying, 'Inasmuch as you did it to the least of these my brethren you did it to me.'

LEADER   The carol is hymn number 92/87

THREE OPTIONAL EXTRA STORIES

Open your home
I don't think I should ever have known the bitterness of loneliness myself if it were not for my time in the Army. My first Christmas Day in khaki gave every promise of being utter misery. Santa Claus doesn't come round and fill your stocking in the Army. It is the orderly sergeant who comes around – with other ideas on his mind!

Breakfast was all gloom; most of the men in the platoon were in a hangover from the night before. Dinner was worse. It was good food spoilt by foul cooking. The officers actually waited on us (!) but they seemed to think that the only thing we wanted came out of barrels. The bawdy stories were worse than ever. I was sick in my soul, and left the mess with the food untasted, to mooch around the streets for the rest of the day. One could at least think about Bethlehem.

And then it happened! As I traipsed about in the drizzle I met a civilian who seemed to recognise me. He stopped – hesitated – spoke. Hadn't he seen me in

111

the Methodist church? What was I doing for the day? Would I care to come home and spend the rest of the time with his family? *Would* I? And home I went! His kind wife made me as welcome as her husband. I romped with the children and sat by the fire. I ate so heartily at tea-time that I felt compelled to offer some halting explanation about having had no dinner, and I marked the birth of Jesus where all was light, and love, and joy. I thank God for that experience. It taught me to say 'Come in'.   [W. E. Sangster]

Visit to Father Christmas

I once put Father Christmas to the test and caught him out. I was a very small lad and yet remember being taken by my Mum to Lewis's in Manchester to see Father Christmas in Toyland. We paid our shilling, my sister and I, and when it was our turn, she went first – she always did because she was older than I – and she told the red and white monster what she wanted and I noticed that it was all on her Christmas toy list from home. I was more crafty, even in those days, and asked for something not on my official list. 'What do you want?' boomed this mountain of red flannel and cotton wool which smelt of stale tobacco, glue, and that medicine which Daddy took with soda when he had a cold. I said, 'Roller skates, please.'

No one else knew about the skates. It was just between me and him alone. It was not on my written list. I never did get my roller skates, so I never learned to skate, but it confirmed what I had already suspected. He was a fake, he was not the real Father Christmas who came up with the goodies on Christmas Day. He was a sales gimmick – an employee of Lewis's toy department. I had further discoveries yet to make on this entire subject.

But imagine you are taken to meet Christ and not Santa Claus. You have a chance to ask him for anything. You tell him more about yourself by what you ask for than by the way you ask. When beggars come near Christ they do not ask for toys, money, food or even security. In Scripture they ask to be given their sight, they ask to be given healing

strength and eternal life. God is not Father
Christmas, never ask him for things to test him out.
You are coming to your Maker. Ask him for what you
cannot live without – here or in eternity. This
Christmas ask God for things that only God can give.

[Frank Cooke]

The Gifts of the Magi was written by William Sydney
Porter who lived from 1862 to 1910. He wrote many
short stories under the name of O. Henry, but none
more poignant than this. It was about a young newly
married American couple who lived at the turn of the
century and were very poor. The young wife was
proud to be Mrs James Dillingham Young but on
Christmas Eve all she had was 1 dollar and 78 cents
and she wept for she could not buy a present for her
husband Jim. Jim earned only 20 dollars a week and
the only thing of value he possessed was his father's
gold watch which had no chain. Della had lovely
flowing hair which was so long it reached below her
knees. She went to a shop which made wigs and sold
her hair to them. She came out with twenty dollars
but without all her lovely long hair. She went to the
jeweller and bought a platinum watch chain for Jim.
It cost 21 dollars. She hurried home.

At 7 p.m. Jim was due home but he was late that
night. She heard him come into the apartment from
the door below and panicked. She tried to cover her
short hair with a scarf. 'Please God make him think
I'm still pretty,' she cried.

Jim came in and stared at her. She was so afraid.
'Don't look at me like that. I sold my hair to buy you a
Christmas present,' she said. 'You say your hair has
gone,' gasped Jim, as if in a trance. He put a small
package down on the table and said, 'I love you with
or without your long hair', and she opened the parcel
– her Christmas present from Jim was the set of
combs she had always wanted. They were
tortoiseshell with jewelled rims exactly right for
containing long flowing hair. She assured her new
husband that her hair would grow again.

'Now,' she said picking up the watch chain, 'let me pu
this on your gold watch and see how splendid it looks.'

'But I sold the watch to buy the combs,' he said and
there we leave them laughing and crying in each
other's arms.

For smaller gatherings

Preparation

1 Select the appropriate items from the foregoing presentation, adapt
   them where necessary and arrange with those taking part to be fully
   briefed.
2 If you choose one of the discussions be clear about the aim and ahead
   of time 'prime the pump' by arranging that a couple of the children
   explain
   (a) some of their Christmas giving secrets or
   (b) how they feel about the way we all spend Christmas in our locality.
3 If you choose to invite a guest speaker on any of the subjects below
   make sure you explain how much time is available and do arrange for
   the speaker to be met at the school office (or Head's study), escorted
   to the correct place and be properly and courteously introduced and,
   at the close, thanked.

Additional material

1 Discussion subjects
   (a) on the subject 'What we are giving this Christmas', the aim being
       to encourage and stimulate thoughtful giving of Christmas gifts.
   (b) on the subject 'How do you think we could celebrate Christmas
       better than we do?'
2 A guest speaker recommended (and vetted!) on any seasonal subject
   such as
   (a) Christmas in Poona (or Panama),
   (b) Christmas in prison or prisoner-of-war camp,
   (c) Christmas in hospital (as a patient or nurse),
   (d) Christmas away from home.

Follow-up ideas

1 If any of the items selected grips and stirs the interest of the group
   discuss with them how they might take some *practical* steps to be of
   help in the area of interest.
2 You may wish to use the story 'The coming of the King' (in Extra
   material).

114

19   Towards Easter – the Cross

For larger assemblies

Leader's preparation

1   Read through the presentation and select those items you intend to use.
2   Arrange for the musical duet or solo or choir if possible and if natural, and arrange also the musical accompaniment for the hymns.
    If you have the musical duet or solo or choir arrange for the singers to be standing ready to sing at the beginning of the assembly and able to sit down immediately, so as not to interrupt the theme by intrusive noise and too much movement. Choice of music should be made by the music leader but could be one of the following pieces:
    (a) Were you there when they crucified my Lord?
    (b) My song is love unknown
    (c) O sacred head, sore wounded.
3   The reader of 'The Killing' by Edwin Muir should rehearse carefully in order to bring out the meaning.
    This reading could be accompanied by taped background of dramatic music faded up and down at prearranged intervals, e.g. Gustav Holst's 'Mars, the bringer of War' from the Planets Suite, or the opening of Shostakovich's Fifth Symphony, or any other starkly suitable background music.
4   The parable teller should tell it as a story and as he ends, the music (as used above) should be faded in for a few seconds, maintain volume and then fade.
5   The reading from John is a long one. If there is time to read it all and it is well rehearsed and well read it is deeply moving. The text could be copied out and marked up for a narrator and the other voices.

Assembly presentation

LEADER	Greetings! This morning we look towards one event which still baffles men and splits history in two.
SOLO OR GROUP	'Were you there when they crucified my Lord?' (verses 1 and 2) (See assembly leader's preparation 2.)

READER 1 That was the day they killed the Son of God
On a squat hill-top by Jerusalem.
Zion was bare, her children from their maze
Sucked by the demon curiosity
Clean through the gates. The very halt and blind
Had somehow got themselves up to the hill.

After the ceremonial preparation,
The scourging, nailing, nailing against the wood,
Erection of the main-trees with their burden,
While from the hill rose an orchestral wailing,
They were there at last, high up in the soft spring
  day.
We watched the writhings, heard the moanings, saw
The three heads turning on their separate axles
Like broken wheels left spinning. Round *his* head
Was loosely bound a crown of plaited thorn
That hurt at random, stinging temple and brow
As the pain swung into its envious circle.
In front the wreath was gathered in a knot
That as he gazed looked like the last stump left
Of a death-wounded deer's great antlers. Some
Who came to stare grew silent as they looked,
Indignant or sorry. But the hardened old
And the hard-hearted young, although at odds
From the first morning, cursed him with one curse,
Having prayed for a Rabbi or an armed Messiah
And found the Son of God. What use to them
Was a God or a Son of God? Of what avail
For purposes such as theirs? Beside the cross-foot,
Alone, four women stood and did not move
All day. The sun revolved, the shadow wheeled,
The evening fell. His head lay on his breast,
But in his breast they watched his heart move on
By itself alone, accomplishing its journey.
Their taunts grew louder, sharpened by the
  knowledge
That he was walking in the park of death,
Far from their rage. Yet all grew stale at last,
Spite, curiosity, envy, hate itself.
They waited only for death and death was slow
And came so quietly they scarce could mark it.
They were angry then with death and death's deceit.

I was a stranger, could not read these people
Or this outlandish deity. Did a God
Indeed in dying cross my life that day
By chance, he on his road and I on mine?

LEADER   Hymn number 84/81/3

LEADER   In the days of the Roman empire many thousands of
people were executed by being nailed up on crosses
and left to die in agony.
    The terrible magnetism of the death of Jesus is not
in pain suffered heroically but in that this particular
person should die like that and why.
    Here is a story, a modern parable by Frank Cooke:

READER 2 The planet was dying of pollution, radiation and
starvation and the leaders selected a man and a
woman to be put into suspended animation capsules
and sent off in a space probe till the sensors selected a
planet able to sustain them with air, food and water.

    After thousands of years the space ship landed on a
distant planet and the computer awakened the man
and the woman and they stepped out into a
dazzlingly beautiful world: distant mountains, purple
and snow-layered hills covered in trees and foliage of
many greens, sparkling rivers streaming through rich
green valleys and gathering round them in innocent
curiosity animals of all shapes, sizes and colours, and
all of them friendly to the new arrivals and to each
other.
    The man and the woman began to make a home for
themselves, plant food, gather fruit and kill some of
the animals for meat.
    After a few years had passed the man, the woman
and their two children born to them lived in a brown
area round their spaceship for all their grass had
receded, the animals had run away and the trees had
been cut down. Years passed and became centuries,
and the invaders travelled all over the lovely planet
but wherever they went they took with them death
and destruction, not only by what they did, but there
was a killing disease in their blood which infected
them, their children and every kind of life on the

planet. More years passed and soon it was clear to the wisest of the descendants of the original man and woman that this planet also would be doomed unless they could find an antidote to the killing infection in their blood.

When they were at their wits' end, a strange craft appeared and landed near the mountains. In it was a being who was just like them except for one thing. He did not have the infected blood. He was healthy and full of descriptions of where he had come from. He enthralled them with his stories, but their wise men knew that they needed his life blood to make serum which would, by being injected, make antibodies in them to resist the killing madness, so they and their planet would be saved from destruction.

They decided to catch him secretly and begin the terrible experiments but much to their surprise he seemed to know what they were about to do and, instead of running away, he gave himself to them willingly. When they had used him up they put his body back into his spaceship and decided to make a monument of it. But before they could, just as suddenly as it had landed, it took off into the blue and disappeared in a blaze of power, leaving them aghast.

(Optional reading as time allows: John 18:12 to 19:42, possibly selecting the verses to be read – see preparation 5 – and using two or more readers.)

Then the detachment of soldiers with its commander and the Jewish officials arrested Jesus. They bound him and brought him first to Annas, who was the father-in-law of Caiaphas, the high priest that year. Caiaphas was the one who had advised the Jews that it would be good if one man died for the people.

Simon Peter and another disciple were following Jesus. Because this disciple was known to the high priest, he went with Jesus into the high priest's courtyard, but Peter had to wait outside at the door. The other disciple, who was known to the high priest, came back, spoke to the girl on duty there and brought Peter in.

'Surely you are not another of this man's disciples?' the girl at the door asked Peter.

He replied, 'I am not.'

It was cold, and the servants and officials stood around a fire they had made to keep warm. Peter also was standing with them, warming himself.

Meanwhile, the high priest questioned Jesus about his disciples and his teaching.

'I have spoken openly to the world,' Jesus replied. 'I always taught in synagogues or at the temple, where all the Jews come together. I said nothing in secret. Why question me? Ask those who heard me. Surely they know what I said.'

When Jesus said this, one of the officials near by struck him in the face. 'Is that any way to answer the high priest?' he demanded. 'If I said something wrong,' Jesus replied, 'testify as to what is wrong. But if I spoke the truth, why did you strike me?' Then Annas sent him, still bound, to Caiaphas the high priest.

As Simon Peter stood warming himself, he was asked, 'Surely you are not another of his disciples?'

He denied it, saying, 'I am not.'

One of the high priest's servants, a relative of the man whose ear Peter had cut off, challenged him, 'Didn't I see you with him in the olive grove?' Again Peter denied it, and at that moment a cock began to crow.

Then the Jews led Jesus from Caiaphas to the palace of the Roman governor. By now it was early morning, and to avoid ceremonial uncleanness the Jews did not enter the palace; they wanted to be able to eat the Passover. So Pilate came out to them and asked, 'What charges are you bringing against this man?'

'If he were not a criminal,' they replied, 'we would not have handed him over to you.'

Pilate said, 'Take him yourselves and judge him by your own law.'

'But we have no right to execute anyone,' the Jews objected. This happened so that the words Jesus had spoken indicating the kind of death he was going to die would be fulfilled.

Pilate then went back inside the palace, summoned Jesus and asked him, 'Are you the king of the Jews?'

'Is that your own idea,' Jesus asked, 'or did others talk to you about me?'

'Do you think I am a Jew?' Pilate replied. 'It was your people and your chief priests who handed you over to me. What is it you have done?'

Jesus said, 'My kingdom is not of this world. If it were, my servants would fight to prevent my arrest by the Jews. But now my kingdom is from another place.'

'You are a king, then!' said Pilate.

Jesus answered, 'You are right in saying I am a king. In fact, for this reason I was born, and for this I came into the world, to testify to the truth. Everyone on the side of truth listens to me.'

'What is truth?' Pilate asked. With this he went out again to the Jews and said, 'I find no basis for a charge against him. But it is your custom for me to release to you one prisoner at the time of the Passover. Do you want me to release "the king of the Jews"?'

They shouted back, 'No, not him! Give us Barabbas!' Now Barabbas had taken part in a rebellion.

Then Pilate took Jesus and had him flogged. The soldiers twisted together a crown of thorns and put it on his head. They clothed him in a purple robe and went up to him again and again, saying, 'Hail, O king of the Jews!' And they struck him in the face.

Once more Pilate came out and said to the Jews, 'Look, I am bringing him out to you to let you know that I find no basis for a charge against him.' When Jesus came out wearing the crown of thorns and the purple robe, Pilate said to them, 'Here is the man!'

As soon as the chief priest and their officials saw him, they shouted, 'Crucify! Crucify!'

But Pilate answered, 'You take him and crucify him. As for me, I find no basis for a charge against him.'

The Jews insisted, 'We have a law, and according to that law he must die, because he claimed to be the Son of God.'

When Pilate heard this, he was even more afraid, and he went back inside the palace. 'Where do you come from?' he asked Jesus, but Jesus gave him no answer. 'Do you refuse to speak to me?' Pilate said. 'Don't you realise I have power either to free you or to crucify you?'

Jesus answered, 'You would have no power over me if it were not given to you from above. Therefore the one who handed me over to you is guilty of a greater sin.'

From then on, Pilate tried to set Jesus free, but the Jews kept shouting, 'If you let this man go, you are no friend of Caesar. Anyone who claims to be a king opposes Caesar.'

When Pilate heard this, he brought Jesus out and sat down on the judge's seat at the place known as The Stone Pavement (which in Aramaic is Gabbatha). It was the day of Preparation of Passover Week, about the sixth hour.

'Here is your king,' Pilate said to the Jews.

But they shouted, 'Take him away! Take him away! Crucify him!'

'Shall I crucify your king?' Pilate asked.

'We have no king but Caesar,' the chief priests answered.

Finally Pilate handed him over to them to be crucified.

So the soldiers took charge of Jesus. Carrying his own cross, he went out to The Place of the Skull (which in Aramaic is called Golgotha). Here they crucified him, and with him two others, one on each side and Jesus in the middle.

Pilate had a notice prepared and fastened to the cross. It read, JESUS OF NAZARETH, THE KING OF THE JEWS. Many of the Jews read this sign, for the place where Jesus was crucified was near the city, and the sign was written in Aramaic, Latin and Greek. The chief priests of the Jews protested to Pilate, 'Do not write "The King of the Jews", but that this man claimed to be king of the Jews.'

Pilate answered, 'What I have written, I have written.'

When the soldiers crucified Jesus, they took his

clothes, dividing them into four shares, one for each of them, with the undergarment remaining. This garment was seamless, woven in one piece from top to bottom.

'Let's not tear it,' they said to one another.

'Let's decide by lot who will get it.'

This happened that the Scripture might be fulfilled which said, 'They divided my garments among them and cast lots for my clothing.' So this is what the soldiers did.

Near the cross of Jesus stood his mother, his mother's sister, Mary the wife of Clopas, and Mary of Magdala. When Jesus saw his mother there, and the disciple whom he loved standing near by, he said to his mother, 'Dear woman, here is your son', and to the disciple, 'Here is your mother'. From that time on, this disciple took her into his home.

Later, knowing that all was now completed, and so that the Scripture would be fulfilled, Jesus said, 'I am thirsty.' A jar of wine vinegar was there, so they soaked a sponge in it, put the sponge on a stalk of the hyssop plant, and lifted it to Jesus' lips. When he had received the drink, Jesus said, 'It is finished.' With that, he bowed his head and gave up his spirit.

Now it was the day of Preparation, and the next day was to be a special Sabbath. Because the Jews did not want the bodies left on the crosses during the Sabbath, they asked Pilate to have the legs broken and the bodies taken down. The soldiers therefore came and broke the legs of the first man who had been crucified with Jesus, and then those of the other. But when they came to Jesus and found that he was already dead, they did not break his legs. Instead, one of the soldiers pierced Jesus' side with a spear, bringing a sudden flow of blood and water. The man who saw it has given testimony, and his testimony is true. He knows that he tells the truth, and he testifies so that you also may believe. These things happened so that the Scripture would be fulfilled, 'Not one of his bones will be broken', and, as another Scripture says, 'They will look on the one they have pierced.'

Later, Joseph of Arimathea asked Pilate for the body of Jesus. Now Joseph was a disciple of Jesus, but secretly because he feared the Jews. With Pilate's permission, he came and took the body. He was accompanied by Nicodemus, the man who earlier had visited Jesus at night. Nicodemus brought a mixture of myrrh and aloes, about seventy-five pounds. Taking Jesus' body, the two of them wrapped it, with the spices, in strips of linen. This was in accordance with Jewish burial customs. At the place where Jesus was crucified there was a garden, and in the garden a new tomb, in which no one had ever been laid. Because it was the Jewish day of Preparation and since the tomb was near by, they laid Jesus there.

LEADER   Hymn number 141/118

LEADER   Let us pray.

Behold the cross of Christ on which the Saviour of the world did hang. Let us worship and bow down before the man crucified who is Lord of all. Lord Jesus Christ, crucified by our human religious blindness, our political expediency, our slogan-chanting mindlessness and by our moral cowardice, have mercy upon us, we beg you.

It is our sins that put you there, our sins that you bore and our sins that you bear away in suffering love, and in humble penitence we worship and adore you.

We lift up before you all who are this day enduring suffering and imprisonment because of their faith in you, all who have taken up their cross to follow you and all who, following you, endure the loneliness of suffering rather than renounce their faith. Lord Jesus Christ, we bow before you and ask you to forgive us and make our lives clean and ready to obey. *Amen.*

READER 1   Jesus said, 'If anyone would come after me he must . . . take up his cross . . .' **(Mark 8:34)**

LEADER   Your cross is the trouble you wouldn't have if you were not a Christian!

123

For smaller gatherings

Preparation

1 Select the appropriate items from the foregoing presentation, adapt them where necessary and brief those taking part.
2 If you intend using the poem and/or the parable from the preceding pages, plan the best way of presenting them. Arrange and allow time for rehearsals.
3 John, chapters 18 and 19 as printed, could become the basis of the 'script' in which the narrator, different speaking parts and crowd noises are read by the group as a Play Reading. If you decide to do this every pupil will need a copy of the text to mark the various parts and crowd scenes.
4 If there is a talented music group they might be asked to rehearse and then present a rock gospel song of their own choice to suit the occasion.

Additional ideas

1 Part four of the video of Franco Zeffirelli's *Jesus of Nazareth* is readily available from most video shops. As it lasts over an hour it would require a special viewing period. If this is shown, a short break might be arranged followed by a brief discussion period in which the different impressions of the group could be shared.
2 Although quite old now *The Man born to be King*, the play cycle written for radio by Dorothy L. Sayers, is still excellent material and not dated; from it the play sequence *Man of Sorrows* is an excellent script for a group to perform as a play reading after some, but not too much, preparation and rehearsal. The play has so many character parts that the whole group could be involved as cast and crowd. The group leader should read the author's directions and character sketches provided and suggest how the parts be read. It is not necessary to aim at a faultless presentation as it is read by the group for the group only.
3 See also 'The cost' (in Extra material).

Follow-up idea

Encourage volunteers from the group
(a) to find out about special services being held locally on Good Friday;
(b) to arrange for those services to be attended by one or two volunteers each who would prepare a report on their impressions of the service;
(c) after Easter to report back their impressions to the whole group.

20   Resurrection mystery

For larger assemblies

Leader's preparation

1   Read through the presentation and select those items you intend to use. See also 'Homecoming' (in Extra material).
2   Prepare two readers for the Scripture passages and rehearse them. A further reader could be briefed and rehearsed to read 'The Ballad of the Bread Man' which should be read in a throw-away style as if *'boom-boom'* followed some of the verses! Do not 'ham it up', however.
3   Arrange for the musical accompaniment for the hymns.
4   Arrange for someone to coach the two characters in the scene from the play so that it is acted well enough to be 'natural'.
5   Read through the prayers, amend them if you wish, and prepare thoughtfully to lead them.

Assembly presentation

LEADER   Greetings!
Today our theme is an awesome mystery. As in judging all mysteries, let us do as they do in a court of law and pay close attention to the eyewitnesses and consider the evidence (well, as much evidence as we have time for).
   Here is one account of the event:

READER 1   Early on the first day of the week, while it was still dark, Mary of Magdala went to the tomb and saw that the stone had been removed from the entrance. So she came running to Simon Peter and the other disciple, the one Jesus loved, and said, 'They have taken the Lord out of the tomb, and we don't know where they have put him!'
   So Peter and the other disciple started for the tomb. Both were running, but the other disciple outran Peter and reached the tomb first. He bent over and looked in at the strips of linen lying there but did not go in. Then Simon Peter, who was behind him, arrived and went into the tomb.

He saw the strips of linen lying there, as well as the burial cloth that had been around Jesus' head. The cloth was folded up by itself, separate from the linen. Finally the other disciple, who had reached the tomb first, also went inside. He saw and believed. (They still did not understand from Scripture that Jesus had to rise from the dead.)

Then the disciples went back to their homes, but Mary stood outside the tomb crying. As she wept, she bent over to look into the tomb and saw two angels in white, seated where Jesus' body had been, one at the head and the other at the foot. They asked her, 'Woman, why are you crying?' 'They have taken my Lord away,' she said, 'and I don't know where they have put him.' At this, she turned around and saw Jesus standing there, but she did not realise that it was Jesus.

'Woman,' he said, 'why are you crying? Who is it you are looking for?'

Thinking he was the gardener, she said, 'Sir, if you have carried him away, tell me where you have put him, and I will get him.'

Jesus said to her, 'Mary.'

She turned towards him and cried out in Aramaic, 'Rabboni!' (which means Teacher) . . . .

Mary of Magdala went to the disciples with the news: 'I have seen the Lord!'   **(John 20:1–16, 18a)**

LEADER   It's awesome when you think that many scholars assessing the evidence focus on that burial headcloth which, they say, means it was still rolled up together. In other words, it had not been taken off; he had gone out of it like taking your hand from a glove leaving it there deflated, empty but intact. No wonder it says that when one disciple saw this he knew that Jesus had risen, but these witnesses were all terrified at what they saw.

Listen to the *earliest* account:

READER 2   'Don't be alarmed,' he said. 'You are looking for Jesus the Nazarene, who was crucified. He has risen! He is not here. See the place where they

laid him.' . . . Trembling and bewildered, the
women went out and fled from the tomb. They
said nothing to anyone, because they were
afraid.   **(Mark 16:6, 8)**

LEADER   Let us sing about this mystery.

Hymn number 63/123

LEADER   When he was writing a letter, attempting to gather
together some of the evidence, the apostle Paul said:

READER 2   Now brothers, I want to remind you of the
gospel I preached to you, which you received
and on which you have taken your stand. By this
gospel you are saved, if you hold firmly to the
word I preached to you. Otherwise, you have
believed in vain.

For what I received I passed on to you as of
first importance: that Christ died for our sins
according to the Scriptures, that he was buried,
that he was raised on the third day according to
the Scriptures, and that he appeared to Peter,
and then to the Twelve. After that, he appeared
to more than five hundred of the brothers at the
same time, most of whom are still living, though
some have fallen asleep. Then he appeared to
James, then to all the apostles, and last of all he
appeared to me also . . .   **(I Corinthians 15:1–8a)**

LEADER   Let us pray.

Almighty God, we stand amazed at the mystery that
Jesus, your Son, who was killed, buried and then
sealed in a guarded cave, should rise from the dead,
victorious over sin and death and the grave. Deliver
us from ignoring what we do not understand and
rejecting evidence just because it seems fantastic.
Enable us to face the challenge of the living one who
dies and the dying one who lives, for the sake of
Jesus Christ our Lord. *Amen.*

READER 3   Mary stood in the kitchen
Baking a loaf of bread.
An angel flew in through the window.
'We've a job for you,' he said.

'God in his big gold heaven,
Sitting in his big blue chair,
Wanted a mother for his little son.
Suddenly saw you there.'

Mary shook and trembled,
'It isn't true what you say.'
'Don't say that,' said the angel.
'The baby's on its way.'

Joseph was in the workshop
Planing a piece of wood.
'The old man's past it,' the neighbours said.
'That girl's been up to no good.'

'And who was that elegant fellow,'
They said, 'in the shiny gear?'
The things they said about Gabriel
Were hardly fit to hear.

Mary never answered,
Mary never replied.
She kept the information,
Like the baby, safe inside.

It was election winter.
They went to vote in town.
When Mary found her time had come
The hotels let her down.

The baby was born in an annexe
Next to the local pub.
At midnight, a delegation
Turned up from the Farmers' Club.

They talked about an explosion
That made a hole in the sky,
Said they'd been sent to the Lamb & Flag
To see God come down from on high.

A few days later a bishop
And a five-star general were seen
With the head of an African country
In a bullet-proof limousine.

'We've come,' they said, 'with tokens
For the little boy to choose.'

Told the tale about war and peace
In the television news.

After them came the soldiers
With rifle and bomb and gun,
Looking for enemies of the state.
The family had packed and gone.

When they got back to the village
The neighbours said, to a man,
'That boy will never be one of us,
Though he does what he blessed well can.'

He went round to all the people
A paper crown on his head.
Here is some bread from my father,
Take, eat, he said.

Nobody seemed very hungry.
Nobody seemed to care.
Nobody saw the god in himself
Quietly standing there.

He finished up in the papers.
He came to a very bad end.
He was charged with bringing the living to life.
No man was that prisoner's friend.

There's only one kind of punishment
To fit that kind of a crime.
They rigged a trial and shot him dead.
They were only just in time.

They lifted the young man by the leg,
They lifted him by the arm,
They locked him in a cathedral
In case he came to harm.

They stored him safe as water
Under seven rocks.
One Sunday morning he burst out
Like a jack-in-the-box.

Through the town he went walking.
He showed them the holes in his head.
Now do you want any loaves? he cried.
'Not today,' they said.

LEADER   That's the challenge of the resurrection. The poem was 'The Ballad of the Bread Man' by Charles Causley. Listen now to this scene by John Masefield. It tells of a conversation between a centurion and a Roman lady in Jerusalem about AD 33. The two characters are Procula, the Roman lady, and Longinus, the Roman centurion.

PROCULA   'Centurion, were you at the killing of that teacher today?'

LONGINUS   'Yes, lady.'

PROCULA   'Tell me about his death.'

LONGINUS   'It is hardly fit hearing for you, my lady . . .'

PROCULA   'Do not tell it all, then, but tell me what he said.'

LONGINUS   'The people were mocking him at first, and he prayed God to forgive them. He said: "Father, forgive them, for they know not what they do . . ."'

PROCULA   'Was he suffering much?'

LONGINUS   'No, lady. He wasn't a strong man. The scourging must have nearly killed him. I thought he was dead by noon, and then suddenly he began to sing in a loud voice that he was giving back his spirit to God. I looked to see God come to take him. He died singing. Truly, lady, that man was the Son of God, if one may say that . . .'

PROCULA   'What do you think the man believed, centurion?'

LONGINUS   'He believed he was God, they say.'

PROCULA   'What do you think of that claim?'

LONGINUS   'If a man believes anything up to the point of dying on the cross for it, he will find others to believe it.'

PROCULA   'Do you believe it?'

LONGINUS   'He was a fine young fellow, my lady; not past middle age. And he was all alone and defied all the Jews and all the Romans, and, when we had done with him, he was a poor broken-down thing, dead on the cross.'

PROCULA   'Do you think he is dead?'

LONGINUS   'No, lady, I don't.'

PROCULA   'Then where is he?'

LONGINUS   'Let loose in the world, lady, where neither Roman nor Jew can stop his truth.'*

LEADER   Let us pray.

In the midst of human cruelty, sin and death we celebrate the victory of Christ the conqueror of them all.

In the midst of oppression and tyranny we celebrate the victory of vulnerable, unchanging love.

In the midst of military might we celebrate the power of unarmed, undefended courage.

In the midst of human helplessness we celebrate the salvation of God.

Lord, we marvel at the mystery of the resurrection, we rejoice in it and praise you for its majestic message to our world. *Amen.*

Now, here, in a word, is a great man's greatest ambition. It was the apostle Paul who had one ambition; he tells us of his greatest desire when he says:

READER 1   'I want to know Christ and the power of his resurrection.'   **(Philippians 3:10a)**

LEADER   Hymn number 125/2/19

*From *The Trial of Jesus*, 'Youth at Worship', published Methodist Youth Department

For smaller gatherings

Preparation

1 Select the appropriate items from the foregoing presentation, adapt them where necessary and arrange with those taking part to be fully briefed.
2 Invite two Christian guests to come and be quizzed by the group on such questions as: 'Why I believe in the resurrection of Christ.'
    If you do,
    (a) ensure that they understand that they are to answer honestly and briefly the question put,
    (b) ensure that the group is briefed to be courteous to their guests,
    (c) arrange for guests to be met, escorted to the venue, properly thanked afterwards and escorted back to the main door by which they entered.

Additional ideas

1 If two willing (and able) volunteers agree, give them a copy of *Who moved the stone*? by Frank Morison (Faber & Faber). Their brief is that at an agreed future assembly they will present a digest of the argument of this book which began as a repudiation of the resurrection and well into his research the author was persuaded by the evidence to rewrite it as a case presented for the truth of the resurrection.
2 See also 'Well?' (in Extra material).

Follow-up idea

If you have the nerve and your group has some humble, sensitive and polite people in it, discuss with them the possibility of interviewing different church leaders in your area with the aim of reporting back to the group at a later assembly. The brief would be a questionnaire on such matters as
(a) If the resurrection were found to be untrue would it make any difference to your church?
(b) What do you believe about the resurrection?
(c) In what sense is Jesus alive today?

21 Towards Whitsun

For larger assemblies

Leader's preparation

1 Read through the presentation and select those items you intend to use.
2 Arrange for two readers and for their rehearsal and enlist a different 'storyteller' for the parable.
3 Arrange for the musical accompaniment for the hymns.
4 The poetry needs to be read deliberately and slowly, perhaps commented upon, and then repeated. Each poem is short enough to do so.
5 This session could well be followed up by inviting a local Christian leader whose faith is vibrant to answer questions on his understanding of God the Holy Spirit.

Assembly presentation

LEADER   Greetings!

Hymn number 80/124/99

LEADER   These days a great many people, not all of them religious, are talking about the Holy Spirit. What do the words 'Holy Spirit' convey to you? Some kind of force like electricity or invisible energy like colourless gas?

     Today we will look at this subject and ask what on earth do Christians mean by saying 'the Holy Spirit *is God*, the third person of the Trinity'?

     Listen.

READER 1   On one occasion, while he was eating with them, he gave them this command: 'Do not leave Jerusalem, but wait for the gift my Father promised, which you have heard me speak about. For John baptised with water, but in a few days you will be baptised with the Holy Spirit.'

(Acts 1:4–5)

This happened fifty days after Passover and in the original language the word for fifty days is Pentecost. Listen again:

READER 2 When the day of Pentecost came, they were all together in one place. Suddenly a sound like the blowing of a violent wind came from heaven and filled the whole house where they were sitting. They saw what seemed to be tongues of fire that separated and came to rest on each of them. All of them were filled with the Holy Spirit and began to speak in other tongues as the Spirit enabled them. . . .

Some, however, made fun of them and said, 'They have had too much wine.'. . .

'These men are not drunk, as you suppose. It's only nine in the morning! No, this is what was spoken by the prophet Joel: "In the last days, God says, I will pour out my Spirit on all people. Your sons and daughters will prophesy, your young men will see visions, your old men will dream dreams."' **(Acts 2:1–4, 13, 15–17)**

LEADER Jesus had told them that the divine vision and power they had seen in him would be available within them as another person who thinks, feels, loves and talks direct to the mind and conscience, invisible yet real. Peter ended his powerful sermon that day with these words:

READER 1 'Repent and be baptised, every one of you, in the name of Jesus Christ so that your sins may be forgiven. And you will receive the gift of the Holy Spirit. The promise is for you and your children and for all who are far off – for all whom the Lord our God will call.' **(Acts 2:38–39)**

LEADER Hymn number 66/51

LEADER In one of the many passages about the Holy Spirit in the Bible the picture of a dove is used. John the Baptist said:

READER 2   'I saw the Spirit come down from heaven as a dove and remain on him. I would not have known him, except that the one who sent me to baptise with water told me, "The man on whom you see the Spirit come down and remain is he who will baptise with the Holy Spirit."'

(John 1:32–33)

LEADER   That symbol of the dove needs to be rescued from the helpless cooing bird of peace in a world of savage wars.

    Listen to the poet T. S. Eliot on this subject:

READER 1   The dove descending breaks the air
With flame of incandescent terror
Of which the tongues declare
The one discharge from sin and error.
The only hope, or else despair
    Lies in the choice of pyre or pyre –
    To be redeemed from fire by fire.
Who then devised the torment? Love.
Love is the unfamiliar Name
Behind the hands that wove
The intolerable shirt of flame
Which human power cannot remove.
    We only live, only suspire
    Consumed by either fire or fire.

LEADER   Let us pray.

    Invisible God, whom we see so perfectly in the person of Jesus, grant us so to put our trust in him that we might begin to know and experience the awesome presence of the Holy Spirit whom Christ promised to all who come to him in faith.
Since our intellects are too blunt, clumsy and earthbound to discern so mysterious a presence, so quicken us we pray that we begin to know the God who reigns above us as the Father; the God who confronts us in the man Jesus, and also the God who seeks to indwell us, even the Holy Spirit. We pray this through Jesus Christ our Lord. *Amen*.

    Listen again to the baffling words of Charles Causley, summing up his 'Ballad of Five Continents'.

READER 2   I am the Prince
I am the lowly
I am the damned
I am the holy.
My hands are ten knives.
I am the dove
Whose wings are murder.
My name is love.

READER 1   Once upon a time there was an Indian Maharajah who was so fabulously wealthy that each year he was weighed against his diamonds.

To celebrate his son's coming-of-age he planned to give a party at his palace and sent out invitations to both the rich and poor of the state over which he ruled. The invitations were unusual in that they stated three specific requests; one was that each guest should bring a present and keep it secret to make it a big surprise on the day. The second was that each gift be made of pure gold, and the third request was that each golden gift must be a receptacle of some kind. All those invited were puzzled but because the eccentric Maharajah was extremely wealthy and powerful they began to comply. One had specially made a tiny doll-sized tea cup; another bought a tiny thimble; still another a tiny golden pill box. 'Well,' they each reasoned, 'it's a receptacle and it's gold so it passes the test.'

One girl who truly loved the Maharajah's son took all her savings, borrowed from her parents and had made an urn of gold on which was inscribed 'With love'.

On the day of the party they all arrived at the palace with their presents wrapped in extra large packages and were shown into a courtyard where the Maharajah met them. He smiled and said, 'Thank you for coming and for being generous enough to bring such golden gifts for my son. He knows nothing of all this and the surprise is not for him, it's for you. Unwrap your gifts now, take them into my treasure store and fill those receptacles to the brim with diamonds and keep them as my gifts to you.'

LEADER Do I need now to add that the different spiritual gifts men receive from God are so often determined by the capacities we offer to him to be filled?

In humility and honesty bring a thimble and he will fill it, a cup, a pail, a pool, an ocean and he will fill them to overflowing.

We cannot 'stage-manage' the presence and power of God the Holy Spirit. We can only ask Jesus to open us up and fill us.

Hymn number 5/60

For smaller gatherings

Preparation

1 Select the appropriate items from the foregoing presentation, adapt them where necessary and arrange with those taking part to be fully briefed.
2 If you intend to invite a discussion on the parable, think it through and refer to the additional idea to see if it offers further help.
3 Encourage any pupils with musical skills to play and sing any songs or choruses they may know about God the Holy Spirit.

Additional idea

Imagine you invite a world-famous organist to play and set before him a two-octave organette from Woolworths. Doubtless he would be able to play you a nice tune.

Now imagine you set the same organist before a great five-manual cathedral organ, and ask him to play. The music would blow your mind. The difference would not be the organist, not even the musical notes. The difference would be the capacity of the instrument.

That's the problem God has when he wants us to play his music.

Follow-up idea

Invite different guests as representatives from different churches over three or four days and ask them questions about their understanding of the Holy Spirit. Suggested guests could include a local Roman Catholic, an Anglican, a 'charismatic' community leader and a traditional Free Churchman.

22 God in the world

For larger assemblies

Leader's preparation

1 Read through the presentation and select items you intend to use.
2 If a member of your staff is technically capable of doing it without too much trouble, have him/her set up a TV monitor before the assembly and demonstrate the opening paragraph. Each time the point of balance is made, return to the set and adjust it.
3 Arrange for the two readers to have the text of their readings and the opportunity to rehearse.
4 Arrange for the musical accompaniment for the hymns.

The opening paragraph can be done in one or two ways:
(a) as a simple explanation;
(b) as a practical demonstration with a TV set.
    If one of your staff is capable of arranging for a TV set to be prominently displayed and pre-tuned so that the vertical and horizontal holds can be separately demonstrated in turn and also together, then the opening paragraph would require suitable pauses as your words were demonstrated by the picture-hold.
    In the leader's second and third paragraphs the experiment could be repeated with suitable pauses.

Assembly presentation

LEADER   Greetings!
(Possible demonstration – see leader's preparation)

LEADER   In order to get a full picture every TV set has to be tuned in two ways. It must have a vertical hold which fills the picture from top to bottom (pause) and it must have a horizontal hold which fills the picture from side to side (pause).
    To get a picture you must have both. Listen.

READER 1   Hearing that Jesus had silenced the Sadducees, the Pharisees got together. One of them, an expert in the law, tested him with this question: 'Teacher, which is the greatest commandment in the Law?'

Jesus replied: 'Love the Lord your God with all your heart and with all your soul and with all your mind. This is the first and greatest commandment. And the second is like it: Love your neighbour as yourself.'   **(Matthew 22:34–39)**

LEADER   So if the world is to see God at work among his people there must be, as on a TV set, the vertical hold of God's love coming down and going up (pause) and the horizontal hold of God's love going out to people like ourselves (pause). It's the two together which make a clear picture (pause).
Listen again.

READER 2   So do not worry, saying 'What shall we eat?' or 'What shall we drink?' or 'What shall we wear?' For the pagans run after all these things, and your heavenly Father knows that you need them. But seek first his kingdom *and his righteousness*, and all these things will be given to you as well.   **(Matthew 6:31–33)**

LEADER   There again God's realm is like the vertical hold (pause) and God's righteousness, that is, what is right and just and good, is the horizontal hold (pause). You cannot have a full picture with only one hold.

READER 1   'I believe in loving God, meditating and praying, and I cannot soil my hands dealing with dirty or crooked people. Just leave me alone with God.'

LEADER   That sounds all right, but it can produce blind, religious bigots. They have only a vertical dimension.

READER 2   'I've no time for any God or anything up there. Religion is humanity caring for people like ourselves. Just do your human best, be honest and treat others as you would like to be treated.'

LEADER   That sounds much better until you remember that millions who believe this confess that they have not the will-power nor the motivation to do it and end up looking after themselves first and putting everyone else second or third, and God nowhere. This is horizontal hold alone.
Remember, we need both to get a picture.

Hymn number 18/135

LEADER OR
READER

Prayers

Lord, set me free from myself. I know what I ought to do but I do not do it.

Deliver me from my body which is always hungry in some way and screaming to be satisfied.

Deliver me from my feelings which love and hate, blush and bluster, choke and embarrass me.

Deliver me from my thoughts which are so full of myself, so bored and so sick of pretending.

Lord, deliver me from myself, my blindness and inner hurts for I am so alone, and come in, like sunlight from above, and set me free to walk in the light without fear or shame. *Amen*.

READER 2

In the mountainous regions of North India, where it is very cold, travellers are helped in keeping warm in this way. They take a small vessel, put coal in it, and cover it up. They weave strings around it and, wrapping it with cloth, carry it under their arms. Three men were travelling thus towards the sacred place of Amarnath. One of them saw several others suffering with cold, and, taking the fire out of the vessel, lit a fire so that everyone could get warm. So everyone left the place alive. When they had all to walk in the dark the second man of the party took out the fire in his vessel and lit a torch with it, and helped them all to walk along in safety. The third man of the party mocked them and said: 'You are fools. You have wasted your fire for the sake of others.' 'Show us your fire,' they said to him. When he broke open his vessel there was no fire, but only ashes and coal. With his fire one man had given warmth to others, and another had given light. But the third man was selfish and kept the fire to himself, and it was no use even to him.

In the same way, it is God's will that the fire of the Holy Spirit which we receive should give warmth and light to others and help them to be saved. Many people despise those who spend their health, strength and money for the salvation of others, and call them mad. And yet it is they who will save many and be saved themselves.

LEADER   Hear what the New Testament says in the Letter of James:

READER 1   My brothers, as believers in our glorious Lord Jesus Christ, don't show favouritism. Suppose a man comes into your meeting wearing a gold ring and fine clothes, and a poor man in shabby clothes also comes in. If you show special attention to the man wearing fine clothes and say, 'Here's a good seat for you', but say to the poor man, 'You stand there', or 'Sit on the floor by my feet', have you not discriminated among yourselves and become judges with evil thoughts? . . . If you really keep the royal law found in Scripture, 'Love your neighbour as yourself', you are doing right. But if you show favouritism, you sin and are convicted by the law as law-breakers. For whoever keeps the whole law and yet stumbles at just one point is guilty of breaking all of it. **(James 2:1–4, 8–10)**

LEADER   Hymn number 18/135

For smaller gatherings

Preparation

1   Select the appropriate items from the foregoing presentation, adapt them where necessary and arrange with those taking part to be fully briefed.

2   Well ahead of time arrange for two pupils to read Jesus' prayer in John 17 concentrating on verses 13–19, asking them in the light of this unit's theme to put it in their own words to be discussed by the group.

'I am coming to you now, but I say these things while I am still in the world, so that they may have the full measure of my joy within them. I have given them your word and the world has hated them, for they are not of the world any more than I am of the world. My prayer is not that you take them out of the world but that you protect them from the evil one. They are not of the world, even as I am not of it. Sanctify them by the truth; your word is truth. As you sent me into the world, I have sent them into the world. For them I sanctify myself, that they too may be truly sanctified. **(John 17:13–19)**

3 If you choose to use the additional item arrange for a good reader to have a copy of the poem 'The Recent Crisis' by James Russell Lowell, below, and give him or her the opportunity to rehearse it.
If you wish to lead a discussion on it mark out the lines which to you seem crucial to the discussion of the 'two holds'.

Additional ideas

1 Once to every man and nation comes the moment to decide,
In the strife of truth with falsehood, for the good or evil side –
Careless seems the great Avenger, history's pages but record
One death-grapple in the darkness 'twixt old systems and the word;

Truth for ever on the scaffold, wrong for ever on the throne –
Yet that scaffold sways the future, and behind the dim unknown
Standeth God within the shadow, keeping watch above his own.
Then to side with truth is noble, when we share her wretched crust.

Ere her cause bring fame and profit, and 'tis prosperous to be just;
Then it is the brave man chooses, while the coward stands aside,
Doubting in his abject spirit, till his Lord is crucified,
And the multitude make virtue of the faith they had denied.

New occasions teach new duties: time makes ancient good uncouth;
They must upward still and onward, who would keep abreast with
   truth;
Lo, before us gleam her camp-fires! we ourselves must pilgrims be,
Launch our Mayflower, and steer boldly through the desp'rate winter
   sea,
Nor attempt the future's portal with the past's blood-rusted key.*

2 See also 'Noah now' (in Extra material).

Follow-up idea

For a period of say a term run a 'gallery of greatness' in the form of a wall display to which names are added. The heading is 'They love God and people!' In order to suggest a name, a pupil should read the relevant book, write out a brief digest (to be read by him and the leader) and recommend to the group that the person featured qualifies for inclusion in the modern 'gallery of greatness'. Such names could include, for instance, Mother Teresa of Calcutta, Archbishop Romero, The Mahatma Gandhi.

*Quoted from 'Youth at Worship', published Methodist Youth Department

23   Wanting more and more

For larger assemblies

Leader's preparation

1   Read through the presentation and select those items you intend to use.
2   Prepare two readers by giving them their texts and opportunity to rehearse.
3   If you wish, during the Mick Jagger and the Rolling Stones quotation, the first part of the record 'I can't get no satisfaction' could be played (CBS records).
     If you do this, make sure that the contrasting reading is read powerfully, perhaps even over a suitable tape-recorded music background.
4   Arrange for the musical accompaniment for the hymns.

Assembly presentation

LEADER   Greetings!
One of the richest men in the world, John D. Rockefeller, was asked, 'How much money would it take to be really satisfied?' He answered, 'Just a little bit more.' For some reason we never seem to learn how to be satisfied. The cat purring and relaxed on the mat shows a contentment most human beings never achieve.
Listen:

READER 1   Two men dashed out of an office building in London and each hailed a taxi. The first one said, 'Heathrow Airport quickly' and then sat on the edge of the back seat drumming his fingers on his brief-case and glancing at his watch every minute, all to make the taxi go faster. It took just as long to get there as if he had sat back and read the paper and done the crossword, but he was too anxious. The other man was in just as great a hurry; he got in his taxi and told the driver to hurry to the airport, then sat back and was so completely relaxed that he slept for the whole journey. The driver wakened him, 'Here you are, sir,

Gatwick Airport.' 'But I wanted Heathrow,' he stammered. 'You didn't say,' said the driver. So you have one man who knows where he is going but is rigid with anxiety, and the other who is so relaxed but not clear about his goal.
Listen:

READER 2   'Therefore I tell you, do not worry about your life, what you will eat or drink; or about your body, what you will wear. Is not life more important than food, and the body more important than clothes? Look at the birds of the air, they do not sow or reap or store away in barns, and yet your heavenly Father feeds them. Are you not much more valuable than they? Who of you by worrying can add a single hour to his life? . . .

  'So do not worry, saying, "What shall we eat?" or "What shall we drink?" or "What shall we wear?" For the pagans run after all these things, and your heavenly Father knows that you need them. But seek first his kingdom and his righteousness, and all these things will be given to you as well. Therefore do not worry about tomorrow, for tomorrow will worry about itself. Each day has enough trouble of its own.'

                            (Matthew 6:25–27, 31–34)

LEADER   We will sing hymn number 93/115

LEADER   God always asks why we want more and more. He always asks if we know why we are never satisfied, because we mostly want things not for their own sakes but to try and compensate for a deeper emptiness.
  Listen to a poem by Coventry Patmore.

READER 1   My little Son, who look'd from thoughtful eyes
  And moved and spoke in quiet grown-up wise,
  Having my law the seventh time disobey'd,
  I struck him, and dismiss'd
  With hard words and unkiss'd,
  – His Mother, who was patient, being dead.
  Then, fearing lest his grief should hinder sleep,
  I visited his bed,

But found him slumbering deep,
With darken'd eyelids, and their lashes yet
From his late sobbing wet.
And I, with moan,
Kissing away his tears, left others of my own;
For, on a table drawn beside his head,
He had put, within his reach,
A box of counters and a red-vein'd stone,
A piece of glass abraded by the beach.
And six or seven shells,
A bottle with bluebells,
And two French copper coins, ranged there with
  careful art,
To comfort his sad heart.
So when that night I pray'd
To God, I wept, and said:
'Ah, when at last we lie with trancèd breath,
Not vexing thee in death,
And thou rememberest of what toys
We made our joys,
How weakly understood
Thy great commanded good,
Then, fatherly not less
Than I whom thou hast moulded from the clay,
Thou'lt leave thy wrath, and say.,
"I will be sorry for their childishness."'

LEADER   Let us pray.

Lord, we long to possess more and more yet we enjoy
less and less. We fill our time with frantic and aimless
busyness. We fill our bodies with things which leave
our minds and souls starved and terminally ill. We
even seek animal contentment as if we were merely
animals. Lord, have mercy on us and enable us to
find that which truly satisfies the soul. *Amen.*

Here are two quotations, the former as sung by Mick
Jagger years ago with The Rolling Stones (see
preparation).

READER 2   'I can't get no satisfaction . . . though I try, though I try,
though I try, though I try, I can't get no satisfaction.'
(Fade)

LEADER   And he did try!

READER 1   I have learned to be content whatever the circumstances. I know what it is to be in need, and I know what it is to have plenty. I have learned the secret of being content in any and every situation, whether well fed or hungry, whether living in plenty or in want. I can do everything through him who gives me strength.

(Philippians 4:11b–13)

LEADER   Anyone who is quite content and fully satisfied with beer, bed and bingo has not yet come alive as a human being. Any who know they need more now need to go on to the next stage, leaving behind the craving for things to try to fill a deeper inner need. Let the Old Testament prophet speak to us:

READER 2   Why spend money on what is not bread, and your labour on what does not satisfy? Listen, listen to me, and eat what is good, and your soul will delight in the richest of fare. Give ear and come to me; hear me, that your soul may live. I will make an everlasting covenant with you. . . .

Seek the Lord while he may be found; call upon him while he is near. Let the wicked forsake his way and the evil man his thoughts. Let him turn to the Lord, and he will have mercy on him, and to our God, for he will freely pardon.

(Isaiah 55:2–3a, 6–7)

LEADER   Hymn number 17/20

LEADER   Here is a very short but power-packed poem by Eden Phillpotts:

READER 1   A severed wasp yet drank the juice
Of a ripe pear upon a plate,
And one did idly meditate
What was the use?

Yet round about us, spent and done
With hands already growing cold,
We see half-man still scraping gold
Its uses gone.

For smaller gatherings

Preparation

1 Select the appropriate items from the foregoing presentation, adapt them where necessary and arrange with those taking part to be fully briefed.
2 If you decide to invite a local businessman to speak and answer questions on 'The satisfaction of life', prepare by
   (a) introducing the idea to the group,
   (b) listening to their suggestions and discussing them,
   (c) agreeing on the kind of questions which could be courteously put,
   (d) making clear that the attitude during question time should be one of good-natured and polite inquisitiveness,
   (e) making precise arrangements about time and ensuring that the speaker is met at the door, properly introduced and afterwards thanked with a properly thought-out vote of thanks.

Additional ideas

1 Invite in a 'successful' local businessman who is articulate and ask him to give his life story to date and be willing to answer questions about 'The satisfaction of life'.
2 See also 'The pulley' (Extra material).

Follow-up idea

Investigate if your group would be interested enough to produce volunteers who would help to compile over a number of weeks some case histories of famous people who seem to have made it to the top. It should appeal to budding journalists and prospective TV reporters. They should aim at trying to discover from press reports and articles the true story behind the glitter. The point of such an ongoing exercise would not be 'critical' and fault-finding but an attempt to discover an objective view of what truly makes for 'a good life'.

24   Is anyone there?

For larger assemblies

Leader's preparation

1   Read through the presentation and select those items you intend to use.
2   Arrange for two readers for the Scripture passages and if you think it helpful another reader for the parable 'The bird that talked'. Again it is essential for the readers to have a copy of the text and that they rehearse not only their lines but their presentation and their entrances and exits.
3   Arrange the musical accompaniment for the hymns.
4   You may wish to arrange 'The bird that talked' as a dramatic reading or even a play. If so, you will need to cast the parts of the narrator, Maud, Bill and the choir, and arrange enough rehearsal time.

Assembly presentation

LEADER   Greetings!
Did you hear that marvellous tale told by
some joker or other in which he declared
he had been receiving messages from outer space?
We are quoting from a book. Listen:

READER 1   He needed help to understand them. He claimed that he had persuaded the governments of the world to write across the Sahara Desert in letters each 100 miles long and 70 miles wide, the words 'Please repeat the message'. Months later, in the same language, the message was flashed to earth – 'We were not talking to you.' That story tickled me, and later made me realise that the human race is star-struck. It is fascinated by the thought that there may be some other form of intelligent life out there in the universe.

The success of space odyssey type films and the success of such books as *Chariots of the Gods* and *Return to the Stars* indicates that people everywhere do long to know the answers to such questions as where did our earth come from? Are we unique in an otherwise 'empty' universe? Are the stories of the Bible really visits of astronauts from other worlds, in which case, who made *them* and what is *their* god like?

Space engineers have already dispatched a probe which asks in sign language, 'Is there anyone out there? If so, get in touch with us.' In all this we are crying out in letters one hundred miles high, 'Is there anyone out there; please talk to us.'

The quotation continues:

Now stop and see this. The whole universe itself is one vast message to us. If we can but interpret the language. The message goes like this – 'Listen, I'm talking to you, personally. Look and see what I am saying to you in the heavens and in the created order on earth. Let the starry heavens above and the moral voice of law within fill you with awe and wonder.'

LEADER   No one has ever seen God, no one!

READER 2   That's true. No one has ever seen God because, for one thing, he's invisible to human eyesight!

READER 1   For another thing, God isn't a creature so how can creatures like us grasp him?

LEADER   So we cannot know God or even know about him, unless . . .

READERS 1
AND 2   Unless what?

LEADER   Unless he shows himself to us. Unless he tells us what he is like. That process of human learning is called REVELATION. This is a valid way for human beings to learn. The normal way they learn – so they think – is by discovery, which comes by adopting the three processes
(a) observation,
(b) forming intelligent guesses, and
(c) testing them.
We call those three steps the scientific method. Yet every great discovery comes (usually to those who have done the spade-work) by sudden inspiration.

Eureka is the Greek word for 'I've found it', and that break-through is so often a *revelation* – an act of creation which brings the break-through in our human discovery.

Listen to this:

READER 1   Do you not know? Have you not heard? Has it not been told you from the beginning? Have you not understood since the earth was founded? He sits enthroned above the circle of the earth, and its people are like grasshoppers. He stretches out the heavens like a canopy, and spreads them out like a tent to live in. He brings princes to naught and reduces the rulers of this world to nothing. . . .

Do you not know? Have you not heard? The Lord is the everlasting God, the Creator of the ends of the earth. He will not grow tired or weary, and his understanding no one can fathom. He gives strength to the weary and increases the power of the weak. Even youths grow tired and weary, and young men stumble and fall; but those who hope in the Lord will renew their strength. They will soar on wings like eagles; they will run and not grow weary, they will walk and not be faint.

(Isaiah 40:21–23, 28–31)

LEADER   We shall sing hymn number 32/50

READER 2   The heavens declare the glory of God; the skies proclaim the work of his hands. Day after day they pour forth speech; night after night they display knowledge. There is no speech or language where their voice is not heard. Their voice goes out into all the earth, their words to the ends of the world. **(Psalm 19:1–4a)**

When I consider your heavens, the work of your fingers, the moon and the stars, which you have set in place, what is man that you are mindful of him, the son of man that you care for him? You made him a little lower than the heavenly beings and crowned him with glory and honour.

You made him ruler over the works of your

hands, you put everything under his feet; all flocks and herds, and the beasts of the field, the birds of the air, and the fish of the sea, all that swim the paths of the seas.

O Lord, our Lord, how majestic is your name in all the earth.   **(Psalm 8:3–9)**

LEADER   Let us pray.

Almighty God, whose handiwork is seen streaming through the heavens, whose glory is seen in flower and field and whose quiet thunder is heard in our consciences, we marvel that you have so plainly made yourself known in your word and supremely in Jesus Christ; in what he said, what he did and who he was we can see what you are from all eternity and what you are saying, doing and being.

In his simplicity, authority and power we see your mightiness, in his vulnerability and loneliness on the cross we see your suffering love, and in his resurrection and ascension we see your victory over even the worst that men can do.

Lord, for coming to us in Jesus and speaking to us in syllables of his flesh and blood, we praise you, we worship and adore. Through Jesus Christ our Lord. *Amen.*

And now a parable, 'The bird that talked'.

Bill was a farmer, born and bred. He loved his farm, the animals and especially the birds. He enjoyed the dawn chorus and never grew angry when they swooped on his newly-sown seed; 'plenty for us all' he would say. He admired their alert watchfulness, their industry in foraging for food. So it is not surprising that God used a bird to speak to him!

Now I don't mean that a monstrous parrot swooped down and preached a sermon to him. It happened like this:

READER 1   It was near Christmas and Bill's wife Maud was just leaving to go to the Carols by Candlelight service at church. 'Won't you come, Bill?' 'No,' he said, 'I get nothing out of going. It never rings any of my bells.' 'All right,' she sighed, and kissed him as she left for church.

151

Bill went to inspect his farm buildings to ensure that everything was settled down for the night, for it was very cold. Just near to the barn he was startled by a frantic fluttering at his feet. He flashed his torchlight towards the partly open barn door and saw a wounded bird scuttling along the ground. Bill assumed that the cat had had it and although it had escaped was badly injured. Obviously its wing was broken. He decided he would take care of it and nurse it back to health and then set it free, so he followed it into the barn. It fled between two straw bales and he could not reach it. He moved one; it scurried further into the barn moving like a rag doll on a string and every time Bill got near it it found the strength to scramble into even more inaccessible places.

'You silly little thing,' Bill said under his breath. 'I don't want to hurt you. I want to take care of you, protect you and set you free.'

By now he was sweating and saying to himself, 'If only I could talk to it in a language it could understand. If only I could become a bird . . . but even if I could that wouldn't help. I'd need to be a man as well, because birds can't set broken wings.'

For almost an hour he tried to capture it until finally from a tiny space where it had crawled to hide he gently brought it out, but it was quite dead. Bill wept, partly out of frustration for he wanted only to help it, heal it and set it free. 'If only it had trusted me,' he said to himself, 'but I couldn't get it to understand.'

Bill washed and changed hurriedly for he heard the sounds of a crowd of young people gathering at the front door. He had forgotten that they were coming to sing carols and enjoy mince pies and coffee at the farmhouse. As he went down he heard as if for the first time the words of the carol:

'Pleased as man with men to dwell,
Jesus our Emmanuel.'

Maud saw immediately that something was the matter, for when the group sang

'Light and life to all he brings,
Risen with healing in his wings'

the word wings broke him and he hurried into the kitchen pretending to help Maud with the refreshments. 'What's the matter?' she asked. He replied, 'I'll tell you later, only I've just found out why God found it necessary to come to earth as one of us.'   [Frank Cooke]

LEADER   Hymn number 143/40

LEADER   And now a closing prayer:
Lord, go before us this day and
in our ignorance, enlighten us,
in our weakness, strengthen us,
in our loneliness, befriend us,
in our hardness, soften us,
– When we stumble, hold us with your arm,
– When we fall, lift us to our feet,
– When we pursue evil, bring us to our knees,
– When we reach out to you, reach into us and touch us we pray. *Amen.*

For smaller gatherings

Preparation

1   Select the appropriate items from the foregoing presentation, adapt them where necessary and arrange with those taking part to be fully briefed.
2   You may wish to work out in greater detail the ideas briefly contained overleaf concerning scientific methods of discovery and revelation by illustrating that all scientific method does consist of three steps:
   (a) careful observation (when it is controlled it becomes 'experiment');
   (b) forming an intelligent guess to explain it (called a 'hypothesis');
   (c) testing it to see if it works (called 'proving').
From your own experience some illustrations might spring to mind. Some of these might even be demonstrated on the desk or illustrated on the board.
Revelation is the moment of break-through. 'I've found it!' It seems to come from outside, from beyond. For a fuller treatment of this subject see Arthur Koestler's *Act of Creation*. Thus in all learning there are two ways of knowing. One is human discovery, reaching up by trial and error and perspiration, and the second is inspiration which comes as

illumination and pushes out the frontiers of human knowledge to the next barrier. Both these ways interact and stimulate human beings to new thoughts and new knowledge. Prepare this carefully and the discussion/question time will prove extremely lively and fruitful.

Additional ideas

Depending on the 'character' of your group it might be possible to challenge them to try a personal experiment over a period of days or weeks.

Let them select a subject or issue which they find almost totally bewildering, some area they simply cannot grasp. The challenge is to experiment by
(a) a fresh attempt at re-learning the basics of their problem subject,
(b) pinpointing the points which are not understood and setting them down simply, then
(c) relaxing while the ideas simmer; even going to sleep at night leaving the puzzle as their last thoughts, and
(d) seeing if anything happens as a break-through in their understanding.

Follow-up idea

Make a note in your diary to check from time to time some of the issues raised and selected by you from this unit.

25 Relationships

For larger assemblies

Leader's preparation

1 Read through the presentation and select items you intend to use.
2 Today two leaders might be preferred. Liaise with your co-leader.
3 Choose two readers and provide them and your co-leader with copies of the relevant texts; then rehearse them together.
4 Arrange for the musical accompaniment to the hymn and any other musical item possible and relevant.
5 Consider the possibility of the Scripture reading and/or parables being enacted as brief play-reading presentations. If you decide to do this, ensure that your rehearsals are adequate and include smooth entrances and exits.
6 The following idea may appear to be out of the question, but it is quite possible given a great deal of patience and tact by you, and careful thought and enough time.

   If there has been a school dispute or a local controversy in which two sides have been sharply opposed, perhaps two of the leading opponents could be brought together privately and personally reconciled, even if they still continue to hold opposite opinions. The air could possibly be cleared by their sharing publicly and jointly in some statement or light-hearted demonstration of their reconciliation.

Assembly presentation

LEADER 1 Greetings!
Our theme today is personal relationships. The friendship which unites us to some people and the hatred which severs us from others is as real as the people themselves. I do not mean 'club' or 'tribal' loyalties but real friendships. When any ties are severed everyone can feel the jagged edges of the broken relationship, and unhealed the wound can become infected and poison all other relationships near by.

'Keep your relationships in repair' is good advice, so today we need to take stock of our relationships. Let us try an experiment.

LEADER 2   Get comfortable. Relax all your muscles. Breathe in slowly and hold it, and breathe out and hold it. Breathe in again but don't lift your shoulders. Let all the tension go out of your body. Be still – imagine yourself sunbathing and now close your eyes, and think, am I right with God? What's stopping him coming into my life and bringing his peace? Let go of it and let him in.

Am I right with folk at home? Do I need to apologise, or say 'thank you', or do I need to be a bit more understanding? Is there anyone I hate?

Resolve now to ask for power to forgive. Is there anyone I have wronged? Ask for strength to swallow your pride and resolve to put things right.
(Pause)

LEADER 1   And now a prayer.

Lord, let me be right with you, my heavenly Father, that I can find the strength to be right with others. Forgive and get rid of all my grudges, bitter memories, longings for revenge, all desires to hurt just to get my own back. Drive out these resentments by the healing, restoring force of your love. *Amen.*

LEADER 2   Hymn number 103/65/120

READER 1   For if, when we were God's enemies, we were reconciled to him through the death of his Son, how much more, having been reconciled, shall we be saved through his life!   **(Romans 5:10)**

READER 2   A parable: The Four Sons and the Widow.

A certain wealthy widow had four sons. She wanted them to enjoy themselves while they were still young so she divided up the estate. The youngest son took his share and went to a hippy-type commune in Katmandu and wasted his money on wine, women and drugs.

The second son was indignant at such goings on and spent his days criticising such long-haired drop-outs. He used his share to get a nice sensible flat in town, wear nice sensible clothes, take out nice sensible girls, coming home at a nice sensible time and keeping his mother informed about his nice sensible behaviour.

The next son was fanatically involved with a religious sect and gave away all his money to them and spent his time at meditation meetings with his friends and begging for money from people outside to keep their commune going. He was far too busy in his god's work to bother about his mother and brothers, but occasionally he got his religious friends to pray for them.

The eldest son was a complete disappointment. He went to Katmandu to bring the youngest son home, but he wouldn't join them in their drug trips or sexual habits and so they told him to go home and finally threw him out. Next he went to the religious commune and tried to talk to his brother but his brother tried to convert him by bombarding him with verses and getting all his friends to work on him. When he didn't join them they forced him out because they were sure he had come to spy on them. So he came away to tell his other brother what he'd been trying to do. The other brother exploded, 'You fool. I could have told you all that before you left. Mum has been lonely; I'm the only one who cares. I've sent her flowers and reports on my progress. I've been in to see her myself regularly once a week for a whole hour, sometimes twice. You are wasting your life as you've wasted Dad's money on fruitless journeys.' So the eldest son left and went home.

His mother was there at the gate to meet him, and also his girlfriend who'd waited for him. They hugged each other and cried for quite a while, enough to scandalise the neighbours peeping through the curtains at them, and the three of them went in together to eat and talk and pray and laugh and cry, to enjoy the kind of fellowship the other lads were seeking but had not found.

[Frank Cooke]

LEADER 1   Now here is a parable from the Bible:

LEADERS 1 AND 2
READERS 1, 2, 3   (Taking five parts, as narrator/Jesus, father, the elder and the younger son, and the servant.)

Jesus continued: There was a man who had two sons. The younger one said to his father, 'Father, give me my share of the estate.' So he divided his property between them.

Not long after that, the younger son got together all he had, set off for a distant country and there squandered his wealth in wild living. After he had spent everything, there was a severe famine in that whole country, and he began to be in need. So he went and hired himself out to a citizen of that country, who sent him to his fields to feed pigs. He longed to fill his stomach with the pods that the pigs were eating, but no one gave him anything.

When he came to his senses, he said, 'How many of my father's hired men have food to spare, and here I am starving to death! I will set out and go back to my father and say to him: Father, I have sinned against heaven and against you. I am no longer worthy to be called your son; make me like one of your hired men.' So he got up and went to his father.

But while he was still a long way off, his father saw him and was filled with compassion for him; he ran to his son, threw his arms around him and kissed him.

The son said to him, 'Father, I have sinned against heaven and against you. I am no longer worthy to be called your son.'

But the father said to his servants, 'Quick! Bring the best robe and put it on him. Put a ring on his finger and sandals on his feet. Bring the fatted calf and kill it. Let's have a feast and celebrate. For this son of mine was dead and is alive again; he was lost and is found.' So they began to celebrate.

Meanwhile, the older son was in the field. When he came near the house, he heard music and dancing. So he called one of the servants and asked him what was going on. 'Your brother has come,' he replied, 'and your father has killed the fattened calf because he has him back safe and sound.'

The older brother became angry and refused to go in. So his father went out and pleaded with him. But he answered his father, 'Look! All these years I've been slaving for you and never disobeyed your orders. Yet you never gave me even a young goat so I could celebrate with my friends. But when this son of yours who has squandered your property with prostitutes comes home, you kill the fattened calf for him!'

'My son,' the father said, 'you are always with me, and everything I have is yours. But we had to celebrate and be glad, because this brother of yours was dead and is alive again; he was lost and is found.'

(Luke 15:11–32)

LEADER 1   So the parable of the prodigal son is really the parable of two problem sons and a good father. Here is yet another parable but you may need to ponder this short story to see what it is saying to us.

READER 1   It's not fair!

A certain Texas oil millionaire who had no wife and children became quite attached to two of his workmen whom he had employed in the early days of his company, which by now had become a vast international business empire. One of the young men worked like fury from dawn until midnight, seven days a week, all through the year. Everything he did was reported to the owner. Far too busy to marry, he qualified in engineering and company law and as the company had grown he had a finger in every pie and was the most feared and respected director in the whole world-wide organisation.

The other man continued to do the same sort of job he had done at the beginning. He married and had three children but hardly a day passed without the owner of the company dropping in to chat or romp with the children or just sit and talk and sip tea. One day, the owner called the two men to his office and explained that in his will he was leaving the whole company and all his fortune to both of them equally. Once outside, the first man said to the second, 'It's not fair! I've worked my fingers to the bone, built up this vast company while you've done nothing. You've no ambition, you don't deserve more than a few dollars from the old man.' The other one replied, 'Yes, that's absolutely true. It's just that he seems to like me the way I am.'

[Frank Cooke]

For smaller gatherings

Preparation

1 Select the appropriate items from the foregoing presentation, adapt them where necessary and arrange with those taking part to be fully briefed.

2 You may wish to encourage a discussion about international relationships; the maintenance of harmonious relationships which is essential to peace and the breakdown of those relationships which leads to war.

   This is such a vast subject that it is best to discuss or debate a particular issue in the headlines at the time, being prepared with journalistic statements from each side. If you follow this course, be aware and point out the views which are narrowly sectarian and ask why such beliefs are held.

   The *aim* should be to try and discover the meaning of the phrase: 'Blessed are the peacemakers, for they will be called sons of God.'

(Matthew 5:9)

Additional idea

You may wish to introduce a discussion on how we feel when we have had a row with someone. Points not to be neglected include:

(a) Is it always their fault?
(b) What *does* stop us saying we are sorry?
(c) Is it weakness to admit some blame?
(d) How do you react when your apology is not accepted?
(e) Is one attempt at reconciliation enough?
(f) How do we know when two people have had a row?
(g) Why do *they* think no one else knows?
(h) Is it worthwhile 'making it up' when we know that something is bound to go wrong again soon?
(i) Why is it so easy to see both sides of a row when you are not one of those involved?

Follow-up idea

The Parable of the Prodigal Son as Jesus *didn't* tell it:

And he arose and set out for his home, and when at last he arrived at the door, he banged and there was no response. He stood there in his piteous rags and hunger for a while, and then he knocked again and a third time; and finally a window opened and his father looked out and said: 'Oh! it's you. You're spent up, I suppose. You look a nice beauty. What have you come home for? You've had your share of everything. You know where to come when you're hungry . . . '

And he said: 'Father, I have sinned against heaven and in thy sight . . .', but his father banged the window and left him for a while on the doorstep. Presently, his father opened the door and said: 'You're an utter disgrace to me and to all your relatives. I'm ashamed of you; utterly ashamed. But I'm your father, and I've thought it out, and I am prepared to put you on probation for three months, and if, at the end of three months I can find no fault in you, well, perhaps I'll have it in my heart to give you another start . . .'

That is the Parable of the Prodigal Son as Jesus *didn't* tell it. As you hear me say it, your heart cries out against its falsity. 'Lies!' you say. 'Lies!' And you are right; they *are* lies. 'And while he was yet a long way off his father saw him, and had compassion, and ran and fell on his neck and kissed him.'

No probationary period, you notice. No talk of three months. No, it was instant. It was now! Now! 'The robe,' he cries. 'The ring, the ring, the robe, the robe.' [W. E. Sangster]

26 Catastrophe

For larger assemblies

This unit is a basic ground plan to assist preparation for an assembly on
an occasion of some personal tragedy which has fallen upon the
particular school, or some catastrophe in the news which has deeply
touched both staff and children. Obviously, that particular event would
be the starting-point and the material provided would require selection
and sensitive adaptation in order to be relevant and to assist expression
of the emotional needs of the school.

Leader's preparation

1 Read through the presentation and select those items you intend to
   use.
2 Appoint the readers and give them opportunity to rehearse.
3 Let the opening words be spoken with seriousness but without using
   over-emotive words and gestures. Your model should be that of a TV
   newscaster announcing a disaster clearly, sombrely, factually and
   objectively, before moving on to our natural responses to the disaster.
4 Arrange for the musical accompaniment to the hymns and talk over
   with the pianist/organist/ensemble leader the selection of music to be
   played before, during and after the assembly.

Assembly presentation

LEADER Greetings!
This morning the thoughts dominating our minds are
of (here include a factual unemotional statement of
events).

Our turbulent feelings cry out to *do* something but
here in assembly this morning we can mourn
together and let our hearts and thoughts go out in
prayer for those most affected.

In every age men and women have struggled to
express themselves in the face of natural disasters or
tragedies which have resulted from human causes.
These ancient Psalms were created out of a need to
try and make sense of it and express grief. Listen.

READER 1   As the deer pants for streams of water, so my soul pants for you, O God. My soul thirsts for God, for the living God. When can I go and meet with God? My tears have been my food day and night, while men say to me all day long, 'Where is your God?' . . .

Why are you downcast, O my soul? Why so disturbed within me? Put your hope in God, for I will yet praise him, my Saviour and my God.

(Psalm 42:1–3, 5)

READER 2   I say to God my Rock, 'Why have you forgotten me? Why must I go about mourning, oppressed by the enemy?' My bones suffer mortal agony as my foes taunt me, saying to me all day long, 'Where is your God?' Why are you downcast, O my soul? Why so disturbed within me? Put your hope in God, for I will yet praise him, my Saviour and my God.   **(Psalm 42:9–11)**

READER 1   You have made us a reproach to our neighbours, the scorn and derision of those around us. You have made us a byword among the nations; the people shake their heads at us. My disgrace is before me all day long, and my face is covered with shame at the taunts of those who reproach and revile me, because of the enemy, who is bent on revenge. . . .

Yet for your sake we face death all day long; we are considered as sheep to be slaughtered. Awake, O Lord! Why do you sleep? Rouse yourself! Do not reject us for ever. Why do you hide your face and forget our misery and oppression? We are brought down to the dust; our bodies cling to the ground. Rise up and help us; redeem us because of your unfailing love.

(Psalm 44:13–16, 22–26)

READER 2   Do not fret because of evil men or be envious of those who do wrong; for like the grass they will soon wither, like green plants they will soon die away. . . .

Be still before the Lord and wait patiently for him; do not fret when men succeed in their ways, when they carry out their wicked schemes.

Refrain from anger and turn from wrath; do not fret – it leads only to evil. For evil men will be cut off, but those who hope in the Lord will inherit the land.

A little while and the wicked will be no more; though you look for them, they will not be found. But the meek will inherit the land and enjoy great peace. The wicked plot against the righteous and gnash their teeth at them; but the Lord laughs at the wicked, for he knows their day is coming.   **(Psalm 37:1–2, 7–13)**

READER 1 Why, O Lord, do you stand far off? Why do you hide yourself in times of trouble?

In his arrogance the wicked man hunts down the weak, who are caught in the schemes he devises. He boasts of the cravings of his heart; he blesses the greedy and reviles the Lord. In his pride the wicked does not seek him; in all his thoughts there is no room for God. His ways are always prosperous; he is haughty and your laws are far from him; he sneers at all his enemies. He says to himself, 'Nothing will shake me; I'll always be happy and never have trouble.' His mouth is full of curses and lies and threats; trouble and evil are under his tongue. He lies in wait near the villages; from ambush he murders the innocent, watching in secret for his victims. . . .

Arise, Lord! Lift up your hand, O God. Do not forget the helpless. Why does the wicked man revile God? Why does he say to himself, 'He won't call me to account?' But you, O God, do see trouble and grief; you consider it to take it in hand. The victim commits himself to you; you are the helper of the fatherless. Break the arm of the wicked and evil man; call him to account for his wickedness that would not be found out. . . .

You hear, O Lord, the desire of the afflicted; you encourage them, and you listen to their cry, defending the fatherless and the oppressed, in

order that man, who is of the earth, may terrify
no more. **(Psalm 10:1–8, 12–15, 17–18)**

READER 2 God is our refuge and strength, an ever present
help in trouble. Therefore we will not fear,
though the earth give way and the mountains fall
into the heart of the sea, though its waters roar
and foam and the mountains quake with their
surging.
There is a river whose streams make glad the
city of God, the holy place where the Most High
dwells. God is within her, she will not fall; God
will help her at break of day.
Nations are in uproar, kingdoms fall; he lifts
his voice, the earth melts.
The Lord Almighty is with us, the God of Jacob
is our fortress.
Come and see the works of the Lord, the
desolations he has brought on the earth. He
makes wars cease to the ends of the earth; he
breaks the bow and shatters the spear, he burns
the shields with fire. 'Be still and know that I am
God; I will be exalted among the nations, I will be
exalted in the earth.'
The Lord Almighty is with us; the God of Jacob
is our fortress. **(Psalm 46)**

LEADER Hymn number 1/24/104

READER 3 On this planet there are two kinds of catastrophe: one
kind is caused by natural processes over which we
have no control, such as volcanic eruptions,
earthquakes, tornadoes and storms.

LEADER In courts of law these are often referred to as 'Acts of
God', simply because no human being could be
blamed for them. We should not blame God either.
The conditions which cause them are the same factors
which provide all the conditions for life on earth. We
cannot have one without the other.

READER 3 The other kind of catastrophe is man-made. Men are
always cruel, stupid, unjust and greedy. Humans do
terrible things to each other. These include the acts
which men deliberately plan and execute, such as

cold-blooded murder, terrorist bombings and savage cruelty to men, women and children, even animals, birds and sea creatures.

LEADER   Some disasters are man-made but not deliberately planned. We might call them unintentional disasters or appalling accidents.

Take an example. An airliner crashes and explodes. It is without question a terrible disaster, but what caused it? Was it struck by lightning, or even by a meteorite?

READER 1   Nobody could be blamed for that. It is outside human control.

LEADER   Or was it an instrument failure or pilot error? Or had it run out of fuel or had some mechanic or designer made a mistake over some detail?

READER 1   If so, someone had caused that disaster, but not deliberately. Nevertheless, they are held to be responsible for their carelessness or laziness.

LEADER   Or was it a bomb hidden aboard, or did some missile shoot it down?

READER 2   That would not only be a disaster but a deliberate crime against humanity. In such an event our outraged sense of justice and anger cry out for someone to be punished.

LEADER   This gives vent to our feelings and sometimes those feelings are boiling with rage. The world was sick with rage at the Nazis' extermination camps in which millions of Jews perished in gas chambers.

READER 3   But when there is no obvious human agent to blame, many people then blame God for allowing such things to happen. Logically, they ought not to include events which arise out of the very laws which make life possible here on earth.

LEADER   A life-sustaining planet sustains many forms of life:
Flies as well as flowers,
Sharks as well as shrimps,
Nature grand and glorious, but also 'red in tooth and claw',
Poisons as well as provisions.

READER 1   A warm earth which feeds and grows living things must now and then quake and erupt as it settles. Weather patterns and changing seasons, sunshine and storm, dales and deserts, golden age and ice age. This is our world, our home.

LEADER   Thus natural disasters are part of the rent we pay for living on this mysterious and vulnerable planet, spinning in space, called earth.

READER 2   Let us pray.

Praise
Almighty Father God, at whose word the universe exploded into light and being, we praise you for the star-spread heavens and for the splendour of this planet earth our home; we praise you for its sparkling life-teeming seas, for its fruitful, life-filled land, for its cloud-capped mountains and its changing seasons, for its windswept skies streaked by winged flight, for men and women, made for unbroken companionship with you our Father, yet unfulfilled and restless, misfits in a world of riches which can never satisfy them wholly.

For putting into our hearts this yearning for our true home we praise and thank you in longing sadness but with grateful hearts, whose joy is in knowing you, and in knowing you loving you, and in loving you growing more like you.

Through Jesus Christ our Lord. *Amen.*

Intercession
Almighty God, whose love and mercy is infinitely greater than our human care, we commend into your eternal keeping the souls of those who have perished so suddenly from the earth. We commend to your mercy those who this day are stricken with grief and horror and know not which way to turn. We commend to your guiding wisdom all who this day must exercise leadership, apportion responsibility and seek justice and truth. Lord, in your mercy, hear our prayer. *Amen.*

Petition
Almighty Father, who weeps over us in our sin and

suffering, move our hearts now and cleanse us from bitterness and hatred, the hunger for revenge and the hypocrisy of self-righteousness that we might love those who hate us and pray for those who despitefully use us, through him who in the agony of being nailed to the cross, prayed 'Father, forgive them for they know not what they do', even Jesus Christ our Lord. *Amen.*

The Lord's prayer
Our Father, which art in heaven, hallowed be thy name. Thy kingdom come. Thy will be done, in earth as it is in heaven. Give us this day our daily bread. And forgive us our trespasses, as we forgive them that trespass against us. And lead us not into temptation; but deliver us from evil. For thine is the kingdom, the power, and the glory, for ever and ever. *Amen.*

LEADER   Hymn number 133/77

LEADER   What did Jesus say about disasters?

READER 1   Now there were some present at that time who told Jesus about the Galileans whose blood Pilate had mixed with their sacrifices. Jesus answered, 'Do you think that these Galileans were worse sinners than all the other Galileans because they suffered this way? I tell you, no! But unless you repent, you too will all perish. Or those eighteen who died when the tower of Siloam fell on them – do you think they were more guilty than all the others living in Jerusalem? I tell you, no! But unless you repent, you too will all perish.'

(Luke 13:1–5)

LEADER   And again,

READER 2   As he went along, he saw a man blind from birth. His disciples asked him, 'Rabbi, who sinned, this man or his parents, that he was born blind?'

'Neither this man nor his parents sinned,' said Jesus, 'but this happened so that the work of God might be displayed in his life.' **(John 9:1–3)**

LEADER   But why, if he is good, doesn't God make it impossible for us to go so wrong and to do such hideous things?

READER 1   To that the answer of the Bible is simply that God wanted *children* not *puppets* which only moved when he pulled the strings, children who can do right and do wrong, and children who can love you or hate you.

LEADER   Finally this morning a question for you to ponder in this story.

READER 2   Once upon a time there was a mother of a really wild boy who worried her to death by the way he lived, spoke, rejected all discipline and learning. He treated girls cruelly, stayed out all night and drove his motorbike like a maniac, thinking in all this he was creating a he-man image for himself. One day he crashed and was taken to hospital where he lay unconscious for days and weeks.

READER 3   His mother sat by his bed day after day and the truth began to dawn on her. He might be like this now for all his years – a cabbage for the rest of his life.

READER 1   One day, a well-meaning but insensitive visitor said, 'At least he won't cause you any more worry now. He can't do any more mad bad things.'

LEADER   'No,' snapped his mother, 'but I'd rather he be well again even if he spat in my face, wouldn't you?'

Hymn number 36/57

For smaller gatherings

Preparation

1   Select the appropriate items from the foregoing presentation.
2   Adapt the readings, prayers, hymns and items to fit in with the needs and sensitivities of your group.
3   If you use the additional idea be sure that the squeamish are warned and that you are prepared!

Additional idea

An assembly topic which may be a little gruesome but helpful in the long term is 'Why is there such a thing as pain?'

The following excerpts may assist a discussion:

Philip Yancey in *Where is God when it hurts?* has one chapter called 'Painless Hell' which emphasises how appalling life would be without pain, for example

(a) Carville, a well-known American doctor, had a famous patient called Stanley Stein (author of *No Longer Alone*) who went blind because of another cruel quirk of Hansen's disease, a form of leprosy. Each morning he would wash his face with a hot washcloth. But neither his hand nor his face was sensitive enough to temperature to warn him that he was using scalding water. Gradually he destroyed his eyes with his daily washing.

(b) One family told a grotesque story about their congenitally insensitive baby daughter who had just grown four teeth. The mother, hearing her laughing and cooing in the next room, went to her expecting to find some new game the child had discovered. The baby had bitten off the tip of her finger and was playing with the blood, making patterns with the drips. Without pain, she had lost the innate sense of self-protection. How do you explain the danger of matches, knives and razor blades to children like this? One seven-year-old picked at her nose until her nostrils became ulcerated.

The only safe environment for a painless person is to stay in bed all day . . . but even that produces bedsores.

(c) Most worthwhile human accomplishments involve a long history of struggle. Would the pleasure be possible without the painful process? The sculptures and paintings of Michelangelo involved years of pain and misery. Anyone who has accomplished something worthwhile in a house, such as building cabinets or planting a garden, knows this truth. The pleasure, coming after the pain, absorbs it. Jesus used childbirth as an analogy; nine months of waiting, intense labour, then absolute ecstasy.

I talked once with Robin Graham, the youngest person in history to sail around the world alone. He started as an immature, searching kid of sixteen. During his three-year voyage, he was smashed broadside by a violent ocean storm, saw his mast snapped in two by a wave, and barely missed total destruction in a waterspout.

He went through such despair in the Doldrums, a windless, currentless portion of the ocean around the Equator, that he completely gave up, doused his boat with kerosene, and set it on fire. (He quickly changed his mind and jumped back in to extinguish the fire with his hands.)

After three years, Robin sailed into Los Angeles harbour and was greeted by boats, banners, crowds, newsmen, honking cars, and blasts from steam whistles. The joy of returning was far different from any other sailing experience he had known. He would never have felt those emotions returning from a pleasure outing off the coast. The pain and agony of his round-the-world trip made possible the exultation of his triumphant return. He left a sixteen-year-old kid and returned a nineteen-year-old man.*

Follow-up idea

If a small group would volunteer they could read *The Problem of Pain* by C. S. Lewis and write a digest of each chapter to be presented at future assemblies. They might read the whole book but give digests on selected chapters, such as: The fall of man, Human pain, Animal pain. A similar treatment could be used on *Where is God when it hurts?* by Philip Yancey.

*published Pickering and Inglis Ltd.

27 You, the universal mystery

For larger assemblies

Leader's preparation

1 Read through the presentation and select those items you intend to use.
2 If you wish to substitute a more up-to-date story than the one of
  Felipe Garza ensure that it contains the same mystery of body-mind-
  soul interaction.
3 Choose your three readers, provide their texts and allow for sufficient
  rehearsal.
4 Arrange for the musical accompaniment for the hymns.
5 Skim through the material for smaller gatherings to see if you prefer
  to use any of that instead.

Assembly presentation

LEADER Greetings!
        Here is a report which appeared in the *Daily Telegraph*
        early in 1986 from their reporter Ian Brodie. The
        headline read:

READER 1 'Death-wish boy's heart saves girlfriend'.

LEADER The report was about two 14-year-olds who attended
        the same school. He was called Felipe Garza and she
        Donna Ashlock. They had been going out together
        for only two months when Donna's heart condition
        became so serious that she would die without a heart
        transplant. The couple were very close to each other,
        the report said.

READER 1 When Felipe learned of Donna's condition he kept
          saying, 'I'm going to die so I can give my heart to
          her.' Felipe had always had excellent health but
          within three weeks he died of a brain haemorrhage.
          His parents, remembering his wish to give his heart
          to Donna, arranged for the transplant which was
          successfully carried out.

          The report went on: 'Donna still does not know that
          Felipe is dead and that she now has his heart'.

LEADER   The report which is summarised here concluded:

READER 1   'Doctors could not explain what caused Felipe's haemorrhage'.

LEADER   Only the brash would call all that a coincidence, for each one of us is a mysterious mixture of thoughts, impulses, drives, instincts, intentions, ideals, loves, hates, muscles, animal energy and spiritual ideals, all mixed up and interacting on each other. You are much more than a clever animal.
Listen to Psalm 139.

READER 2   O Lord, you have searched me and you know me. You know when I sit and when I rise; you perceive my thoughts from afar. You discern my going out and my lying down; you are familiar with all my ways. Before a word is on my tongue you know it completely, O Lord. You hem me in, behind and before; you have laid your hand upon me. Such knowledge is too wonderful for me, too lofty for me to attain. . . .
For you created my inmost being; you knit me together in my mother's womb. I praise you because I am fearfully and wonderfully made; your works are wonderful, I know that full well. My frame was not hidden from you when I was made in the secret place. When I was woven together in the depths of the earth, your eyes saw my unformed body. All the days ordained for me were written in your book before one of them came to be.   **(Psalm 139:1–6, 13–16)**

LEADER   Hymn number 138/22

READER 3   Let us pray.

When I gaze at the heavens, the moon and the stars which you have created, what is man that you are mindful of him? Yet you have made him a little less than yourself, O God, for we were made to be your friends and to enjoy you.
'The starry heavens above and the moral law within' fill us with awe, for we are wonderfully and mysteriously made.
When we look at Jesus we see man as you meant

him to be, in uninterrupted communication with you the heavenly Father, having power over nature, authority over evil and satanic forces, and with power to heal and restore the bodies, souls and minds of men and women.

Lord, by the Holy Spirit, make us more like Jesus, we humbly pray. *Amen.*

LEADER   William Blake wrote this poem called 'The Divine Image':

READER 1   To Mercy, Pity, Peace, and Love
All pray in their distress;
And to these virtues of delight
Return their thankfulness.

For Mercy, Pity, Peace, and Love
Is God, our father dear,
And Mercy, Pity, Peace, and Love
Is Man, his child and care.

For Mercy has a human heart,
Pity a human face,
And Love, the human form divine,
And Peace, the human dress.

Then every man, of every clime,
That prays in his distress,
Prays to the human form divine,
Love, Mercy, Pity, Peace.

And all must love the human form,
In Heathen, Turk, or Jew,
Where Mercy, Love and Pity dwell
There God is dwelling too.

LEADER   Hymn number 68/16

LEADER   These are some of the things that some other people have said about you, such as George Orwell in *Animal Farm*:

READER 2   'Man is the only creature that consumes without producing.'

LEADER   And again,

READER 3   'The creatures outside looked from pig to man and from man to pig and from pig to man again; but already it was impossible to say which was which.'*

*From 'Animal Farm', by George Orwell published Secker (Martin) and Warburg Ltd.

LEADER   Aristotle thought that man was either a beast or a god!

            Charles Lamb wrote:

READER 1   'Man is a gaming animal. He must always be trying to get the better in something or other.'

LEADER   'Man is a political animal,' said Aristotle (the ancient Greek).

READER 2   'Man is the hunter; woman is his game,' wrote Tennyson.

READER 3   'No man is an Island, entire of itself,' wrote John Donne. 'Every man is a piece of the Continent.'

LEADER   So 'man is a social animal', said another; 'a tool-using animal', said another, and when an ancient Greek once defined man as a 'featherless animal' the philosopher plucked a chicken, set it down, and said, 'Behold a man!' – in fact that last phrase strikes a different chord. Listen.

READER 1   Then Pilate took Jesus and had him flogged. The soldiers twisted together a crown of thorns and put it on his head. They clothed him in a purple robe and went up to him again and again, saying, 'Hail, O king of the Jews!' And they struck him in the face.

            Once more Pilate came out and said to the Jews, 'Look, I am bringing him out to you to let you know that I find no basis for a charge against him.' When Jesus came out wearing the crown of thorns and the purple robe, Pilate said to them, 'Here is the man!'   **(John 19:1–5)**

LEADER   Or, as in the Authorised Version, 'Behold the man!' A real man, the only real man he had ever seen! That's how Christians think of Jesus – as the only truly human being who ever lived.

            In fact, here is a puzzle for you:

READER 2   Did Jesus perform miracles, signs and wonders over nature, evil spirits and disease, healing the sick and raising the dead because he was truly God, or was it because he was truly and perfectly man: man as God intended him to be?

LEADER   H. E. Fosdick, a famous American preacher who died in 1969, once said that chemists might analyse a man as follows:

READER 3   Five feet ten inches tall and weighing one hundred and fifty pounds, and consisting of enough fat to make seven bars of soap, enough iron to make a nail of medium size, enough sugar to fill a shaker, enough lime to whitewash a chicken-coop, enough phosphorus to make twenty-two hundred match tips, enough magnesium for a dose of magnesia, enough potassium to explode a toy cannon, together with a little sulphur. And they say that these chemical elements at current market rates are worth about ninety-eight cents.*

LEADER   Is a man an accidental collision of atoms going it blind? Many are content to leave this mystery with the words of the Bible:

READER 1   So God created man in his own image, in the image of God he created him; male and female he created them. . . . When God created man, he made him in the likeness of God. He created them male and female; at the time they were created, he blessed them and called them 'man'.

(Genesis 1:27; 5:1b–2)

LEADER   Hymn number 85/73

LEADER   Go into this day in peace. Be courageous, cling to what is good, do not seek to return evil for evil, encourage the weak, stand by the handicapped or unpopular, treat all others you meet as made by God. Honour the Father by loving and serving Jesus in the strength of the Holy Spirit. *Amen.*

For smaller gatherings

Preparation

1 Select the appropriate items from the foregoing presentation, adapt them where necessary and arrange with those taking part to be fully briefed.

2 If possible in three minutes, a sympathetic science teacher might be invited to open up a mystery of human heredity by drawing a dot on

    *From 'Adventurous Religion', published SCM Press Ltd.

the board and tracing the heredity mixture back only as far as grandparents to indicate how each person at conception is a totally unique being.

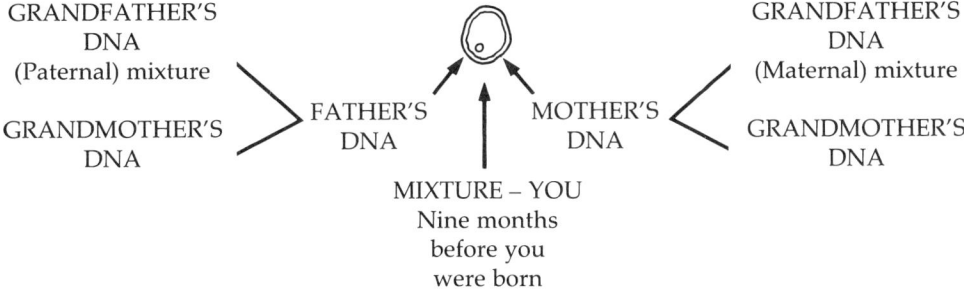

GRANDFATHER'S DNA (Paternal) mixture

GRANDMOTHER'S DNA

FATHER'S DNA

MOTHER'S DNA

GRANDFATHER'S DNA (Maternal) mixture

GRANDMOTHER'S DNA

MIXTURE – YOU
Nine months
before you
were born

Additional ideas

1   What a monstrous spectre is this man, the disease of the agglutinated dust, lifting alternate feet or lying drugged with slumber, killing, feeding, growing, bringing forth small copies of himself; grown upon with hair like grass, fitted with eyes that move and glitter in his face; a thing to set children screaming; and yet looked at nearlier, known as his fellows know him, how surprising are his attributes! Poor soul, here for so little, cast among so many hardships, filled with desires so incommensurate and so inconsistent, savagely surrounded, savagely descended, irremediably condemned to prey upon his fellow-lives: who should have blamed him had he been of a piece with his destiny and a being merely barbarous? And we look and behold him instead filled with imperfect virtues: infinitely childish, often admirably valiant, often touchingly kind; sitting down, amidst his momentary life, to debate of right and wrong and the attributes of the Deity; rising up to do battle for an egg or to die for an idea; singling out his friends and his mate with cordial affection; bringing forth in pain, rearing with long-suffering solicitude his young. To touch the heart of the mystery, we find in him one thought, strange to the point of lunacy: the thought of duty; the thought of something owing to himself, to his neighbour, to his God; an ideal of decency, to which he would rise if it was possible; a limit of shame, below which, if it be possible, he will not stoop.   [Robert Louis Stevenson]

2   See also 'The pulley' (Extra material).

Follow-up ideas

1   Arrange for willing pupils to read biographies of individuals in history (both ancient and modern) who developed into great

characters. Ask the pupils to write a digest of the life-story and
present it to the group on a suitable occasion.

2   By birth St Martin of Tours was a Hungarian, having been born at
Sabaria, a town of Upper Pannonia during the fourth century AD. His
parents were not Christians; his father was an enthusiastic soldier,
who rose to high rank. His supreme wish was that his son should
follow in his footsteps.

When quite a child St Martin's father was moved to Italy. It was
there that the boy received his first education, and there the Spirit
first touched his childish heart. As a little lad of ten, he made the great
adventure of a visit to a Christian church. There he asked to be
enrolled among the catechumens, but it was not until he was eighteen
that the way became clear for him to fulfil the greatest wish of his
heart and be baptised. Three out of those eight years of waiting were
occupied in compulsory military service.

Martin loved soldiers, but he loved Jesus more. At the time his
regiment was 'somewhere in France' on the Somme, where the feet of
British legions since have stood. It was winter, and Martin was riding
with his regiment through the snow and slush into the city of
Amiens. Crowds had gathered to watch the soldiers coming in, worn
and weary, with sodden equipment, perishing with cold, in spite of
thick, warm military cloaks and uniform. As they pass through the
city gate a young officer dismounts. He has seen among the crowd a
poor man, well-nigh naked, blue with the cold, holding out a
trembling hand for alms to buy bread. The officer flings off his cloak,
and, having drawn his sword, he cuts the cloak in two – gently and
courteously he wraps one half of it round the shivering shoulders of
the beggar. Sulpicius says that he had nothing else to give. Perhaps a
great laugh goes up as the crowd see the surprised old beggarman
decked out in the smart purple-blue cloak, and Martin, laughing with
the rest, wraps the other half around himself, remounts, and rides on.

That night as he lay asleep in his billet, he saw a vision. He saw the
half of a military cloak. And he heard a voice which bade him look
well at it, and asked him if he had seen the cloak before. And as he
looked upon it he expected to see beneath it the features of his
shivering friend at the city gate, but he saw the figure of no
beggarman, but the strong and gracious face and form of Jesus
himself. And as in adoring silence Martin listened for the voice to
speak again, the laughing crowd of peasants seemed changed into
groups of the heavenly host. He heard the voice of joy and health,
and united with the mirth of angels he heard the voice of Jesus
saying, 'Martin, yet a catechumen, has clothed me with his garment.'*

*From 'Lectionary of Christian Prose' compiled A. C. Bouquet, published Longman Green and Co. Ltd.

28 'Knowitallitis'

For larger assemblies

Leader's preparation

1   Read through the presentation and select those items you intend to use.
2   Select your readers, give each a copy of the text and time to rehearse.
3   Arrange for the accompaniment for the hymns.
4   If you decide to use the demonstrations, for the first one have a well-briefed assistant plus a board and chalk, or thick marker and a large sheet of paper, or simply draw the two circles yourself as you explain.

For the other two, one of the science teachers could easily reproduce on the board or on a sheet a graph of sound waves and, if possible, the electronic device which makes sounds too high as well as too low for the human ear. The narrow band on the graph indicates our unaided hearing range.

The same message can be repeated by a graph of light waves.

Assembly presentation

LEADER   Greetings!
Imagine that you have been brought up in a primitive tribe deep in the Amazon jungle and know nothing of civilisation. Your father is suddenly seized with a screaming pain in the stomach and you know that he will soon die because you have seen other people die in agony like this.

A strange being suddenly appears wearing clothes all over his body. You'd have killed him instantly but he has a weapon which fires instant death. You had heard from another tribe that such magic is terrifyingly powerful. Imagine this weird being then talking into a little box in his hand. In a few moments a giant metal bird, roaring in ear-splitting din and hovering over the clearing, then slowly comes down, its wings stirring a windstorm around you. Another covered being with black saucered eyes gets out of the huge bird, takes his outer eyes off and the two creatures begin putting your father inside the bird's belly. Your attempts to stop them end with them putting a rope around you and putting you in the bird too! You are suddenly flying above the trees at tremendous speed and you are so terrified you cannot think.

Suddenly, the bird comes gently to earth and a gang of white-coated fiends pick up your father and put him on a long plate as if they are going to eat him alive, your father fainting in shock. They take you into a huge building which is cooler than the heat outside and as they are trying to sit you down, a door is left open and through a space in the wall you see two of them cutting your father open with a knife, while others hold pipes at his mouth. What demented demons these creatures are! By now, you are screaming with fear at their devilish cruelty. How could any of the strange figures explain to you that they were making your father better? You wouldn't have believed them because all you had ever learned about life was being torn apart before your eyes. But then, you wouldn't have known enough to understand, would you? And none of us know all that much even now compared with the mysteries still to be explored.

Listen.

READER 1   Where is the wise man? Where is the scholar? Where is the philosopher of this age? Has not God made foolish the wisdom of the world? For since in the wisdom of God the world through its wisdom did not know him, God was pleased through the foolishness of what was preached to save those who believe. Jews demand miraculous signs and Greeks look for wisdom, but we preach Christ crucified: a stumbling block to Jews and foolishness to Gentiles, but to those whom God has called, both Jews and Greeks, Christ the power of God and the wisdom of God. For the foolishness of God is wiser than man's wisdom, and the weakness of God is stronger than man's strength.   **(I Corinthians 1:20–25)**

LEADER   Hymn number 53/69

LEADER   A film released in 1985 called *Cocoon* told the story of visitors to this earth from a distant planet who had come to recover some of their own kind left here 10,000 years ago. The visitors looked human enough but under the skin they seemed to be made of light! Even the pool in which they kept their cocoons became so charged that it proved to be a fountain of youth. The young man liked one of the visitors, a girl, and he wanted to be able to express affection in the only way he knew. The visitor, however, expressed her attraction by exploding in light and power all around him and reaching him in ways different from the animal energy he had always known. Even the dolphins in the sea knew far more than any human being!

Yes, it was only a film but one of its lessons is clear: 'There are more things in heaven and earth, Horatio, than are dreamt of in your philosophy', as Shakespeare said.

READER 2   Let us pray.

Lord, deliver us from the ignorance which despises what it does not understand and which condemns anything because it is unfamiliar.

Deliver us from the ignorance which wants to put others right while remaining blind to our own stupidities.

Deliver us from the prejudices which we pretend are convictions.

Deliver us from self-conceit which thinks itself always to be right, from the self-deceit which describes every event as if it were the central controlling figure and from the self-pity which we recognise in others but cannot see in ourselves.

Lord, in our blindness, grant us vision,
Lord, in our ignorance, open our minds,
Lord, in our arrogance, break us,
Lord, in our emptiness, fill us and by your royal humility make us teachable, open-minded, and able to be filled with wonder. Through Jesus Christ our Lord. *Amen.*

LEADER   Hymn number 46/97

Demonstration

I am now going to try to prove to you that the more we know the more we don't know, the more we learn the more we need to learn. (Assistant to draw a small circle on the board or large sheet.)

Let this small circle represent all we humans knew a thousand years ago and all around it what we didn't know.

Now look how much more we know about technology, medicine and a million things today. (Assistant draws a much larger circle around the other.)

Notice that as the area of our knowledge expands so the area of our ignorance expands also. We are now in touch with a much greater area of what we don't know than we were a thousand years ago.

In all learning the only proper attitude is one of humility, for there are vast mysteries in this world and beyond it that we do not know anything about and have not the physical equipment to receive this knowledge, so we invent 'tools' to widen our range. (The Science Department has rigged up these two graphs.)

TEACHER 1   I am going to play some high-pitched sound and bring it lower. Will you indicate when you hear it? And then when you stop hearing it?

TEACHER 2   (Display) Here is a graph of light waves. This little segment in the middle is the extent of our unaided vision. (Demonstrates the light waves we cannot see because they are too long or too short.)

LEADER   There is so much that we do not know. It is as if the whole cosmos were saying to us: 'Now, don't get too clever – you are still in your infancy!' Listen to this – it draws a line between wisdom and cleverness and pictures wisdom as a woman trying to get a city to hear what she is saying.

READER 1   Does not wisdom call out? Does not understanding raise her voice? On the heights along the way, where the paths meet, she takes her stand; beside the gates leading into the city, at the entrances, she cries aloud: 'To you, O men, I call out, I raise my voice to all mankind. You who are simple, gain prudence; you who are foolish, gain understanding.' . . .

Choose my instruction instead of silver, knowledge rather than choice gold, for wisdom is more precious than rubies, and nothing you desire can compare with her.

I, wisdom, dwell together with prudence; I possess knowledge and discretion. To fear the Lord is to hate evil; I hate pride and arrogance, evil behaviour and perverse speech. Counsel and sound judgment are mine; I have understanding and power. By me kings reign and rulers make laws that are just; by me princes govern, and all nobles who rule on earth. I love those who love me, and those who seek me find me. . . .

I walk in the ways of righteousness, along the paths of justice, bestowing wealth on those who love me and making their treasuries full. . . .

Listen to my instruction and be wise; do not ignore it. Blessed is the man who listens to me, watching daily at my doors, waiting at my doorway. For whoever finds me finds life and receives favour from the Lord. But whoever fails to find me harms himself; all who hate me love death. **(Proverbs 8:1–5, 10–17, 20–21, 33–36)**

LEADER   A parting shot:
'Some men are wise,
Some are otherwise.' (Anon.)

For smaller gatherings

Leader's preparation

1 Select the appropriate items from the foregoing presentation, adapt them where necessary and arrange with those taking part to be fully briefed.
2 You may be able to set up much more elaborate demonstrations than those simple aids in the presentation, but the point still remains that what we see, hear and know is a narrow slot compared with what is to be known.

Additional ideas

1 Have two of your keen students volunteer to obtain the life story of George Washington Carver from the library, read it and then at an agreed date present the amazing story to the group in digest form (Extra material).

Follow-up ideas

There are so many videos available on the mysteries of the world that it would be impossible to compile a list. Nevertheless, selection can be made from BBC and other productions on the world seen through an electron microscope, or the universe seen through a telescope, or the world photographed by heat-sensitive cameras, etc.

29 The spoiler

For larger assemblies

Leader's preparation

1 Read through the presentation and select those items you intend to use.
2 If you decide to use the playlet or some adaptation of it it is vital that the three participants know their lines, are well rehearsed and have also practised a smooth entrance and exit. The argument should be natural, each cutting the others off.
3 Arrange for the two readers to have their texts and time to rehearse and if you think fit arrange for another person to conduct the prayers instead of reader 1.
4 Ensure that the musical accompaniment for the hymns is arranged.

Assembly presentation

LEADER   Greetings!
Hymn number 72/39

LEADER   Everyone agrees about this, something has gone wrong! There is no doubt about it. Everyone who thinks, writes, speaks about our world, even through the centuries, agrees that something on earth is wrong, seriously wrong. The disagreements begin when we start to say *what* it is that is wrong – even more when we start to say how we can try to put things right! For example:

PLAYLET

CHARACTER 1   I'm a Marxist! I know what's wrong with the world.

CHARACTER 2   I'm a depth psychologist! I know what's wrong with the world.

CHARACTER 3   I'm an eastern mystic! I know what's wrong with the world.

CHARACTER 1   We Marxists know that what's wrong is the unequal distribution of this world's resources, and political revolution is the only way to change it.

CHARACTER 2	We psychologists know that what's wrong is the effects of harmful conditioning of our subconscious minds and animal drives when we were small, and knowing our true selves is the only way to change things.
CHARACTER 3	We mystics know that what's wrong is the materialism of the world. This world is illusion. The only reality is our intuitive union with the universal soul. Only getting rid of all worldly desire will change things.
CHARACTER 1	That's rubbish, you flower-loving idiot . . .
CHARACTER 2	You shut up, you red Bolshevik . . .
CHARACTER 3	Gentlemen, please no fisticuffs . . . Love and peace . . .

(CHARACTERS 1, 2, 3 — each interrupting (stop as leader interrupts, and all sit down)

LEADER   Stop. As I said, they all agree something is wrong, but disagree about what it is that is wrong with the world and what will put it right.

So it is unlikely that what I say will appeal to everyone, but I'll try to offer a solution different from these others. Let's go back to a time before the trouble started, well according to the Bible anyway . . .

READER 1   Then God said, 'Let us make man in our image, in our likeness, and let them rule over the fish of the sea and the birds of the air, over the livestock, over all the earth, and over all the creatures that move along the ground.'

So God created man in his own image, in the image of God he created him, male and female he created them.

God blessed them and said to them, 'Be fruitful and increase in number; fill the earth and subdue it. Rule over the fish of the sea and the birds of the air and over every living creature that moves on the ground.'

Then God said, 'I give you every seed-bearing plant on the face of the whole earth and every tree that has fruit with seed in it. They will be yours for food. And to all the beasts of the earth

186

and all the birds of the air and all the creatures
that move on the ground – everything that has
the breath of life in it – I give every green plant
for food.' And it was so.

God saw all that he had made, and it was very
good.   **(Genesis 1:26–31a)**

LEADER   What went wrong then? This is the root of the matter.
Listen.

READER 2 'You will not surely die,' the serpent said to the
woman. 'For God knows that when you eat of it (*the
fruit*) your eyes will be opened, and you will be like
God, knowing good and evil.'   **(Genesis 3:4–5)**

LEADER   Forget for a moment that it is the serpent talking and
see that the Bible tells us that at first everything was
good and what went wrong was human beings
wanting to be their own God. This has corrupted
everything at source so that no system can work
properly. C. S. Lewis put it this way:

READER 1 There is one vice of which no man in the world is free;
which everyone in the world loathes when he sees it
in someone else. I have heard people admit that they
are bad-tempered, or that they cannot keep their
heads about girls or drink, or even that they are
cowards. I do not think I have ever heard anyone
who was not a Christian accuse himself of this vice.
There is no fault which makes a man more unpopular
and no fault which we are more unconscious of in
ourselves. The vice I am talking of is Pride or Self-
Conceit. It was through pride that the devil became
the devil: pride leads to every other vice; it is the
complete anti-God state of mind.

LEADER   He invites us to try a test. Listen.

READER 2 How much do I dislike it when other people snub me,
or refuse to take any notice of me, or shove their oar
in, or patronise me, or show off?

The point is that each person's pride is in
competition with every one else's pride. It is because
I wanted to be the big noise at the party that I am so
annoyed at someone else being the big noise. Pride
gets no pleasure out of having something, only out of

having more of it than the next man. We say that people are proud of being rich, or clever, or good-looking, but they are not. They are proud of being richer, or cleverer, or better-looking than others.

The sexual impulse may drive two men into competition if they both want the same girl. But a proud man will take your girl from you, not because he wants her, but just to prove to himself that he is a better man than you.

What makes a pretty girl spread misery wherever she goes by collecting admirers? Certainly not her sexual instinct; that kind of girl is quite often sexually frigid. It is pride. Pride is competitive by its very nature.

The Christians are right: it is pride which has been the chief cause of misery in every nation and every family since the world began. Other vices may sometimes bring people together; you may find good fellowship and jokes and friendliness among drunken people or unchaste people. But pride always means enmity – it is enmity. And not only enmity between man and man, but enmity to God.*

LEADER   So that would explain why none of us ever had to learn to lie or cheat or envy or hate – it came naturally to us. We have to learn how to be true and fair and generous and loving. This we need to pray about. Let us pray now.

READER 1   You may wish to join me at the end of each phrase by saying out loud, if you mean it – 'Lord, deliver us, we pray'.
From our own self-deceiving hearts, which explain away our lies, our lusts and our laziness,
     Lord, deliver us, we pray.
From denouncing other people's sins while excusing our own,
From always wanting to be popular rather than honest and from cherishing the hurts inflicted on us while forgetting the pain we have caused,
     Lord, deliver us, we pray.
From the self-importance which always demands centre-stage,

*From 'Mere Christianity' by C. S. Lewis, published Fontana

From the self-righteousness which never admits it is wrong, and from the self-pity which can weep but only for itself,

> Lord, deliver us, we pray.

From delighting in poisonous gossip and other people's sins,
From displaying the acid in our souls by our untamed tongues and from talking even when we have nothing to say,

> Lord, deliver us, we pray.

Let your deliverance come to us, O Lord, by the invasive power of your Holy Spirit, that he may show us how selfish we are, how we may be sorry enough to change and willing for the Holy Spirit to make us more like Jesus and less like we are now. Through Jesus Christ our Lord. *Amen.*

LEADER   The big problem with our pride is that we cannot put ourselves right. If my problem is my pride and I pick myself up and make myself better, I then start to glow with self-satisfaction and pride at my achievement, so that my new condition is worse than the one I had left!

READER 2   We all know about that awful character who 'Put in his thumb and pulled out a plum, and said "What a good boy am I!"'

And if you are prepared to think about it, it's been said that 'the world is full of self-made men who worship their creator'. Well, go on, think about it!

LEADER   I can no more cure myself of pride than I can pick myself up with my own shoe laces or operate on my own brain, but there is outside help available which you will see if you take particular notice of the words of the hymn.

Hymn number 83/56

LEADER   Jesus once told a devastating story which goes right to the heart of all this self-righteous business and how God sees it:

READER 1   To some who were confident of their own righteousness and looked down on everybody else, Jesus told this parable:

'Two men went up to the temple to pray, one a Pharisee and the other a tax collector. The Pharisee stood up and prayed about himself: "God, I thank you that I am not like all other men – robbers, evildoers, adulterers – or even like this tax collector. I fast twice a week and give a tenth of all I get."

'But the tax collector stood at a distance. He would not even look up to heaven, but beat his breast and said, "God, have mercy on me, a sinner."

'I tell you that this man, rather than the other, went home justified before God. For everyone who exalts himself will be humbled, and he who humbles himself will be exalted.' **(Luke 18:9–14)**

LEADER   Hymn number 29/112

For smaller assemblies

Leader's preparation

1   Select the appropriate items from the foregoing presentation, adapt them where necessary and arrange with those taking part to be fully briefed.

2   Read through the additional material and if you intend to use it decide on who will read, making sure all are well rehearsed. You may wish to make 'The Everlasting Mercy' into the main feature of one assembly. In this case obtain copies of John Masefield's poems from the library and arrange for a digest of the story to be presented by a narrator who would link the chosen quotations which should be read dramatically by another reader.

It is a long work and thoughtful editing and time to rehearse are essential.

3   The extra lesson also needs careful expression in its presentation.

4   If you decide to use follow-up idea 1 then the best preparation is for everyone to have his or her own private confession-sheet to keep.

Additional ideas

NARRATOR   John Masefield's ballad 'The Everlasting Mercy' is a great story and this small excerpt is given to whet the appetite for more. It is the story of a wild fighting man called Saul Kane and begins:

READER   From '41 to '51,
I was my folk's contrary son;
I bit my father's hand right through
And broke my mother's heart in two.

From '51 to '61
I cut my teeth and took to fun.
I learned what not to be afraid of
And what stuff women's lips are made of;
I learned with what a rosy feeling
Good ale makes floors seem like the ceiling.

From '61 to '67
I lived in disbelief of heaven.
I drunk, I fought, I poached, I whored,
I did despite unto the Lord.
I cursed, 'twould make a man look pale,
And nineteen times I went to jail.

NARRATOR   He went from bad to worse: it's not a pretty tale, and then into the pub and his screaming drunkenness came a Quaker, Miss Bourne, who accepted his challenge, poured out his drink on to the floor and told him about Jesus. Something broke in Saul's brain and this is how he felt:

READER   I did not think, I did not strive,
The deep peace burnt my me alive;
The bolted door had broken in,
I knew that I had done with sin.
I knew that Christ had given me birth
To brother all the souls on earth, . . .
And every bird and every beast
Should share the crumbs broke at the feast.

O glory of the lighted mind.
How dead I'd been, how dumb, how blind.
The station brook, to my new eyes,
Was babbling out of Paradise;
The waters rushing from the rain
Were singing Christ has risen again.
I thought all earthly creatures knelt
From rapture of the joy I felt.

The narrow station-wall's brick ledge,
The wild hop withering in the hedge,
The lights in huntsman's upper storey
Were parts of an eternal glory.
Were God's eternal garden flowers,
I stood in bliss at this for hours.

O glory of the lighted soul,
The dawn came up on Bradlow Knoll,
The dawn with glittering on the grasses,
The dawn which pass and never passes.
'It's dawn,' I said, 'and chimney's smoking,
And all the blessed fields are soaking.
It's dawn, and there's an engine shunting:
And hounds, for huntsman's going hunting.
It's dawn, and I must wander north
Along the road Christ led me forth.'

Additional Bible reading can be introduced by something like: Listen to this piece of soul-searching from a man struggling with his own self-centredness, and how he can be rescued from it.

We know that the law is spiritual; but I am unspiritual, sold as a slave to sin. I do not understand what I do. For what I want to do I do not do, but what I hate I do. And if I do what I do not want to do, I agree that the law is good. As it is, it is no longer I myself who do it, but it is sin living in me. I know that nothing good lives in me, that is, in my sinful nature. For I have the desire to do what is good, but I cannot carry it out. For what I do is not the good I want to do; no, the evil I do not want to do – this I keep on doing. Now if I do what I do not want to do, it is no longer I who do it, but it is sin living in me that does it.

So I find this law at work: When I want to do good, evil is right there with me. For in my inner being I delight in God's law, but I see another law at work in the members of my body, waging war against the law of my mind and making me a prisoner of the law of sin at work within my members. What a wretched man I am! Who will rescue me from this body of death? Thanks be to God – through Jesus Christ our Lord. **(Romans 7:14–25a)**

Follow-up ideas

1   The General Confession is said by millions of people every day. You may find it helpful to use it in the following way (see preparation 4). Ask each one to write down in their own words what each part means to them and keep it for their own future private use.

  Almighty and most merciful Father; We have erred, and strayed from thy ways like lost sheep.

  * *What things do I do wrong just by doing what all the others do?*

  We have followed too much the devices and desires of our own hearts.

  * *What is my main temptation?*

  We have offended against thy holy laws.

  * *What moral laws do I break which make me feel guilty?*

  We have left undone those things which we ought to have done; And we have done those things which we ought not to have done; And there is no health in us.

  * *Precisely what right things have I left undone?*
  * *And what bad things have I done deliberately?*
  * *And am I glad or sorry about all this?*

  But thou, O Lord, have mercy upon us, miserable offenders. Spare thou them, O God, which confess their faults. Restore thou them that are penitent; According to thy promises declared unto mankind in Christ Jesu our Lord.

  * *Am I sorry enough to want to give up my sins?*
  * *Do I want God to forgive me?*

  And grant, O most merciful Father, for his sake; That we may hereafter live a godly, righteous and sober life. To the glory of thy holy Name. *Amen.*

  * *Do I want to live for God or for myself?*

  Lord, take me as I am and make me what I ought to be. *Amen.*

2   Arrange for a showing of the Academy award-winning film of the Nazi Holocaust called 'Genocide' (90 minutes) available from Religious and Moral Education Press.

30 The world's most widespread anguish

For larger assemblies

Leader's preparation

1 Read through the presentation and select the items you intend to use.
2 Choose your readers and rehearse with them.
3 Arrange the musical accompaniment for the hymns.

Assembly presentation

LEADER	Greetings! Hymn number 96/3
LEADER	Today we are going to look at the world's most widespread anguish. It knows no bounds or barriers. It attacks children, young people, the old and the middle-aged. Crowds only make it worse; it attacks saints and sinners. It invades prisons and palaces, gloomy bed-sitters and glamourous homes. You see it etched in the faces of widows and divorcees, and here and there, even in newly-weds, jet-set business men propping up bars in foreign five-star hotels, students in digs, soldiers in camp, sailors at sea, pop stars, film stars and drop-outs, all can suffer from it and they and millions do. We call it Loneliness. Listen to what more than one person confesses:
READER 1	'I always bid the newscaster goodnight by kissing the TV screen – you see, I've no one else in all the world to kiss.'
READER 2	'There they sprawled all over the filthy floor, a crowd of drug-deadened people unaware that they were even together, for each one was in his or her own self-induced escape, in total isolation from the others.'
LEADER	The man on the radio described the scene:
READER 1	The lady had dropped her purse in the supermarket.

I picked it up, overtook her and to attract her attention took her by the arm and offered her purse back to her. She didn't look at the purse or say 'Thank you' at once. She looked at my hand on her arm and said, 'You are the first person who has touched me in two years.'

LEADER   In our prayers today, after each petition there will be a pause for you to picture someone and ask God to touch and comfort that person.

LEADER (or   Let us pray.
READER 3)

Today, Lord, we pray for all those who are suffering the anguish of loneliness.

Young children who feel isolated from either or both their parents; children who have no brothers or sisters and only imaginary playmates and children who are scorned and rejected by others who gang up against them. (*Pause*)
People who are isolated from others by shyness, fear, deformity, their colour or physical appearance or who are too easily mimicked or pilloried. (*Pause*)
People who are mourning over a lost partner or a lost child or a lost parent. (*Pause*)
People who have gone to the city's bright lights and found only the darkness of people wanting to use them. (*Pause*)
Those who are far from home in the army, navy, airforce, or training to be nurses or police or fire-fighters, and all lonely students. (*Pause*)
For all who live alone, for all who must work alone and for those leaders and politicians whose duty calls them to make drastic and far-reaching decisions and then stand by them through the howling storms of criticism which result. (*Pause*)
For members of the Royal family whose role often of necessity sets them far apart from all others. (*Pause*)
For employers whose task it is to reduce staff aware of the suffering this will cause, (*Pause*)
and for members of trade unions, members of parliament and members of society who act according to what they believe to be right knowing they will be derided and hated. (*Pause*)

For all lepers, victims of AIDS and quarantined, for all in drugged or drunken isolation, and for all condemned to solitary confinement, and for those whose isolation is walled in by blindness, deafness and paralysis. (*Pause*)

Lord, for all the lonely ones we pray this day. Empower us with sensitivity and courage to befriend the friendless, visit the shut-ins and even love the unlovable. Through Jesus Christ our Lord. *Amen.*

LEADER   Hymn number 136/54

LEADER   In the old Hebrew Bible Psalms 42 and 43 were one psalm set in three stanzas. Listen now to the deep cry of the lonely worshipper who sets out three ways in which his downcast spirit is lifted up. These stanzas were set to music for a section of the temple choir to sing:

READER 1   As the deer pants for streams of water, so my soul pants for you, O God. My soul thirsts for God, for the living God. When can I go and meet with God? My tears have been my food day and night, while men say to me all day long, 'Where is your God?' These things I remember as I pour out my soul: how I used to go with the multitude, leading the procession to the house of God, with shouts of joy and thanksgiving among the festive throng.
  Why are you downcast, O my soul? Why so disturbed within me? Put your hope in God, for I will yet praise him, my Saviour and my God.

(Psalm 42:1–5)

READER 2   My soul is downcast within me; therefore I will remember you from the land of the Jordan, the heights of Hermon – from Mount Mizar. Deep calls to deep in the roar of your waterfalls; all your waves and breakers have swept over me. By day the Lord directs his love, at night his song is with me – a prayer to the God of my life.
  I say to God my Rock, 'Why have you forgotten me? Why must I go about mourning, oppressed by the enemy?' My bones suffer

mortal agony as my foes taunt me, saying to me
all day long, 'Where is your God?'

Why are you downcast, O my soul? Why so
disturbed within me? Put your hope in God, for I
will yet praise him, my Saviour and my God.

(Psalm 42:6–11)

READER 1 Vindicate me, O God, and plead my cause
against an ungodly nation; rescue me from
deceitful and wicked men. You are God my
stronghold. Why have you rejected me? Why
must I go about mourning, oppressed by the
enemy? Send forth your light and your truth, let
them guide me; let them bring me to your holy
mountain, to the place where you dwell. Then
will I go to the altar of God, to God, my joy and
my delight. I will praise you with the harp, O
God, my God.

Why are you downcast, O my soul? Why so
disturbed within me? Put your hope in God, for I
will yet praise him, my Saviour and my God.

(Psalm 43:1–5)

LEADER Now hear about the loneliest man who ever lived. He
spent the years of his public work thronged by
crowds pressing in, demanding, pleading, arguing,
accusing, praising him, hating him and not one
understanding him. His family thought he had gone
over the top and tried to coax him home; his group of
friends fell out about who was his favourite; his
enemies set traps for him; the sick, deranged and
possessed gave him no peace, all seeking help from
him.

At the end one of his friends betrayed him and the
others ran away and he was left alone to face a
mockery of a trial, interrogation, torture and then the
most excruciating, lingering death that men could
devise, nailed up, spread-eagled, through wrists and
ankle bones on a cross.

Even this was not the worst. All through this man's
loneliness he had always been aware of the presence
of the invisible one he called 'Abba', 'dear father',
and now even that was removed and he was utterly,
totally alone. Listen.

READER 2   And they crucified him. Dividing up his clothes, they cast lots to see what each would get.

It was the third hour when they crucified him. The written notice of the charge against him read: THE KING OF THE JEWS. They crucified two robbers with him, one on his right and one on his left. Those who passed by hurled insults at him, shaking their heads and saying, 'So! You who are going to destroy the temple and build it in three days, come down from the cross and save yourself!'

In the same way the chief priests and the teachers of the law mocked him among themselves. 'He saved others,' they said, 'but he can't save himself! Let this Christ, this King of Israel, come down now from the cross, that we may see and believe.' Those crucified with him also heaped insults on him.

At the sixth hour darkness came over the whole land until the ninth hour. And at the ninth hour Jesus cried out in a loud voice, '*Eloi, Eloi, lama sabachthani?*' – which means, 'My God, my God, why have you forsaken me?'
(Mark 15:24–34)

LEADER   That is the loneliest man in the world, what a German scholar described as 'The God-forsaken God'.

Hymn number 84/81/141

LEADER   Here are some points to ponder:

READER 1   There is all the difference in the world between loneliness and solitude. Solitude is bliss, loneliness is agony.

READER 2   The cure for your loneliness occurs when you befriend a lonely person.

READER 1   If you now feel lonely, trust someone today and tell them about it.

READER 2   Spare some time today remembering people who do not feel at home even when they are at home.

For smaller gatherings

Preparation

1 Select the appropriate items from the foregoing presentation, adapt them where necessary and arrange with those taking part to be fully briefed.
2 Obtain a copy of the Beatles' recording 'All the lonely people' and set it up ready to play as you need it.
3 If you decide to attempt the follow-up idea first discuss it with the school head and then possibly other members of staff in order to discover the best ways of trying to help with the problems of loneliness in your area.

Additional ideas

Play the tape recording of the Beatles singing 'All the lonely people' and let the group discuss the example of loneliness referred to in the lyrics. Could the group think of better examples of lonely people about whom to write or sing?

Follow-up idea

Depending on your area, it may be possible to sustain a project over a period of a year during which your group attempts to combat various forms of loneliness. So many factors are involved that if you decide to do this you should aim at stimulating a more permanent organisation outside the transient body of children which comprises your group. Perhaps they could help by
(a) Attempting a survey of people who live alone or who seem to be vulnerable and isolated; no names and addresses to be referred to in open discussion.
(b) Let the group discuss ways of obtaining information including, (i) a visit from (or to) one or more of the social workers of the DHSS working in your locality, and (ii) a survey done by the group in which local doctors, ministers, Rotarians, Rotaract, Round Table members, district health visitors and nurses, etc., are asked for information about the problems of loneliness which they encounter.
(c) Let the group discuss the best ways of helping in this problem and of notifying the appropriate social help agency of the needy cases they discover.
Great care is required in such a project that names and addresses of people who live alone are not communicated openly.

Extra material

Forbidden fruit

Once upon a time there was a family of Mum, Dad and two boys who lived in a house in the suburbs which had a very large garden. This garden had a number of apple trees, pear trees and several plum trees but next door's garden had only one apple tree in the middle of an unkempt garden. The apples on that tree always looked nicer than any in their garden. One day, in October, Dad said to the two boys, 'You can pick the apples today if you want to', and then with a wink as he got into the car, 'and you'd better want to!' Mum, who was going shopping, called out, 'And don't go near next door. That dog is dangerous.'

The lads worked for a while, ate some apples, but all the time the apples on next door's tree looked redder and more inviting than any of theirs and the big savage dog roaming next door's garden on a long leash of rope seemed to be a challenge to them. After a while one of the boys leaned over the fence and distracted the dog by shaking a rag at it. It was going frantic. Meanwhile his brother climbed the fence and raided next door's tree, stuffing the apples inside his shirt and his pockets. As he scrambled back over the fence with his spoils the dog saw him and went for him and just managed to get its teeth into his trousers and tore them. When they had stopped laughing the two boys realised that they had to eat or hide next door's apples – they were so different from their own.

Later that day they had dreadful tummy ache through eating too many apples which were not as sweet as they appeared to be. Mum soon discovered the truth and said quietly to Dad, 'But how can we cure them?' Dad said, 'Do you mean from tummy ache or from stealing next door's apples?' Mum said, 'No, from wanting other people's apples.' Dad said, 'Even scaring them by telling the police wouldn't change their desire to steal, would it? Anyway, I'll go next door and have a word with the neighbours.' There was no answer so he went round the back but no one was at home. The dog, made frantic by the two boys, had broken free and it savagely attacked him, biting his arms and legs and even going for his throat. He managed to escape, shut the side gate and stagger home, torn and bleeding. The boys felt terrible when they saw him and in a couple of days Dad was quite ill with a high fever and was rushed into hospital. As they waited outside the ward with Mum one of the lads said tearfully to her, 'I hate next door's apples.' 'And their dog,' said his brother. Mum said nothing but continued to look anxiously through the ward window.

The cost

Once upon a time, in the mountains of human land, a missionary doctor discovered a tribe which was totally blind. They lived their primitive, accident-prone, restricted tribal life in total darkness. Every day someone fell over or off something, so they developed a code of laws to make sure no one would leave anything around to trip anyone up. But children got maimed and killed and men got enraged and lashed out cruelly; no one could help for no one could see – either themselves, their family, their neighbours nor the rich natural world all around. The doctor discovered that their blindness was curable by a simple operation. His hardest task was in convincing them that they needed sight for none of them knew what people, light and colour were, or what water, trees, mountains and sky looked like.

After the first operations, those who could now see went through their own tribe excitedly describing the new world which was the same old world but so gloriously different. Many wouldn't believe them. They thought they were being made fun of, so the sighted ones went into the mountain country and found many other blind tribes and from every valley people came in droves to the doctor to be healed and given this new gift.

Some, however, were not cured because after the operation they followed the advice of the old witch doctor and put animal dung in their eyes, which he said would help recovery. Some had already put pointed bones into their eyes for bravado and decoration and the doctor had nothing to work on. But some, mostly from the first tribe, refused to be treated. They preferred to stay as they were and stumble around in the dark, familiar world of touch. They defended themselves by mocking their sighted brothers saying grim joke things like, 'I can't *see* it at all'; 'Show me and I'll believe'; 'Who do other tribes think they are, taking over our doctor?' 'After all, we had him first'.

In deep sadness, one beautiful young girl (who had had the operation) said to the doctor, 'My husband, I can see him now; he's lovely in spite of his scars but he won't come to you. He says you're only after his money and when I say "But we haven't got any" he says, "He wants us to be his slaves, nothing is free in this world, people don't do all this for nothing." He said he's not going to have his life ruined, he enjoys it too much and the witch doctor agrees with him. What can we do? How can we *make* him see?'

The doctor replied, 'I want him and everyone to see, but there's nothing we can do yet. You can't nag him into coming to see me. Perhaps all these other tribesfolk rejoicing in new-found vision will make him jealous and he'll come to me himself one day ... *providing I'm still here.*'

The girl said in a panic, 'You're not leaving, are you?', and he replied, 'Not immediately, but soon.' As he said this, he stumbled and fell over a chair. 'Your blindness is catching, and I had to get it myself in order to cure you all. Soon it will be time for me to go and once and for all annihilate the disease.'

Noah now

This *jeu d'esprit* was printed in the *Daily Telegraph* and culled from St Margaret's magazine, Addington, Surrey.

The Lord said to Noah, 'Where is the Ark I commanded you to build?' And Noah said, 'Verily I have had three carpenters off sick. The gopher-wood supplier hath let me down – yea, even though the gopher-wood hath been on order for nigh upon twelve months. The damp-course specialist hath not turned up.' And God said to Noah, 'I want that Ark finished before seven days and seven nights.' Noah said, 'It will be so', and it was not so. The Lord said to Noah, 'What seems to be the trouble this time?' Noah said, 'My subcontractor hath gone bankrupt. The pitch for the outside of the Ark hath not arrived. The plumber hath gone on strike. The glazier departeth on holiday to Majorca, yea, even though I offered him double time. Shem hath formed a pop group with his brothers Ham and Japheth. Lord, I am undone.' The Lord grew angry and said, 'What about the animals? Two of every sort I have ordered to come to thee to be kept alive. Where, for example, are the giraffes?'

And Noah said, 'They have been delivered to the wrong address, but should arrive on Friday.' And the Lord said, 'Where are the monkeys and the bears and the elephants and the zebras?' Noah replied, 'They are expected today.' The Lord said to Noah, 'How about the unicorns?' Noah wrung his hands and wept, 'O Lord, Lord, they are a discontinued line. Thou canst not get unicorns for love nor money. Thou knowest how it is.' The Lord said, 'Noah, my son, I know. Why else dost thou think I am causing a flood?'

An eye for an eye

A story for the Christmas season by Henry Francis William Tatham, 1860–1909 (abridged)

Marcus sat by the roadside and nursed his bruised face. . . . Opposite to him his little cottage was burning; down the road the soldiers of the governor were driving off his cow and her calf; in front of the cottage lay chickens dead and wounded, beehives overset, flowers and vegetables trampled and trodden into an indistinguishable mass. By his side his fourteen-year-old daughter crouched sobbing in terror and misery. Marcus spat from his mouth a broken tooth. . . . His fault had been small, and the punishment brutal and severe; and he cursed the governor and vowed vengeance in his heart. . . .

A rude turf hovel on the borders of the great wood, a little plot of land . . . such wild things as he could snare or shoot with his arrows – these gave them shelter and sustenance for a while. But hard times came. The frost bound the earth in an iron grip . . . fuel and bread were well-nigh exhausted. His little daughter came crying to him for food one day. Marcus had just returned from the wood . . . empty-handed. . . . In despair . . . unable to bear his daughter's tears, he started out into the wood.

. . . a great stag came out and passed into an open glade that lay not far in front. . . . There was not a moment to be lost. He set an arrow in the bow, and drawing it to the head, aimed behind the stag's shoulder at the heart. But a twig cracked . . . though the bow twanged and the arrow sped home, it struck but the flank of the deer, and the animal bounded away . . . the arrow sticking into the wound.

Marcus started up in . . . pursuit . . . he soon saw to his grief that the deer had crossed the fence that marked off the part of the forest that was the governor's property.

. . . some thirty yards inside, there lay the deer, seemingly dead. Marcus . . . knew the cruel penalties . . . for one who broke the forest laws. But his daughter was starving; there was no one near to see; after all, he had wounded his quarry fairly on the common ground. With a hasty glance about him, he climbed the fence and went in. . . . the deer was dead. He stooped down to pull out the arrow, and at that very moment he was seized . . . overpowered, and with his hands bound . . . dragged before his enemy, Julian, the governor.

The forest laws were cruel. . . . After a cruel scourging came a worse thing, and Marcus staggered forth, with his hands pressed in agony to the bleeding socket where his right eye had lately been.

Back to his hovel he made his way; and there he would have starved . . . but for the kindness of one of the very men who . . . had seized him in the wood, but had afterwards pitied his sad fate. So he tided over the winter . . . living by hard daily labour . . . and his daughter grew older . . . and became beautiful – alas, too beautiful for her happiness.

For the governor saw her one day, as . . . she went to school to learn . . . of the new faith called Christian that had come into the land. . . . So he made his followers seize the maid and carry her off. The poor girl shrieked and struggled, but her weak efforts were quickly being overpowered when a man came running to her help. It was her father. He held a hatchet. . . . But his axe was of no avail against armed men, and the soldiers, urged by the governor, closed in a circle on him and the girl. He did not hesitate; the fate that would be hers was worse than death, and he struck her one blow, whereat she sank to the ground, and found release.

The governor, mad with rage . . . checked himself and with a cruel smile, 'Thou shalt live,' he said, 'daughterless and eyeless that thou art, thou shalt be handless too. Smite off the hand that struck the blow.'

. . the hand was laid upon the anvil and struck off at the wrist . . . and a red-hot iron that shone in the fire was clapped hissing on the bleeding stump, and stayed the flow of blood. . . . Then they left him fainting in the road.

The Christian Fathers took him up and carried him to their dwelling, and brought him back to life, teaching him also the new faith. . . . But deep down in his heart, whatever the teachings of Christ told him, smouldered the desire for revenge, 'an eye for an eye, a hand for a hand, a tooth for a tooth'.

. . . In Marcus's poor distracted heart there grew a strange desire to see the Lord Jesus, and later by degrees a conviction that he would see him. . . . Meanwhile there came trouble in the land. The governor Julian's oppressions were many and sore and the people hated him. . . . News came of a change of emperor at Rome, his enemies gathered courage and rose against him, and in a little Julian was overthrown, but escaped. . . . Marcus rejoiced at his downfall, yet he longed to hear that some worse thing had befallen him, and was not content that he should escape thus. It was Christmas night . . . Marcus had been working all day in the field . . . he was looking at the stars, when suddenly he was attracted by one that shone with unusual brightness, and what is more, seemed to him to move.

Marcus followed its movements . . . the appearance of Christ came vividly into his mind. And the star, descending, seemed to lead him to a rough thatched building that stood near a farm. He went up to it and pushed the door open, and saw that it was a stable . . . the scent of hay and the breath of oxen, and dimly lighted with a lantern. . . . Then oxen and asses stood meekly in their stalls, as they had stood that night in Bethlehem so many years ago. . . . And Marcus stood and gazed.

Taking down the lantern . . . slowly he went forward to the manger. There was someone lying in it. But it was no innocent child that met the eye of Marcus; no virgin mother sat beside it, no angels folded their wings above. The figure was that of a man, the clothes foul and tattered; the face was pressed in the straw, and one arm covered it. . . . The sleeper

stirred . . . turned his face . . . towards him. And through the dirt . . . and
matted beard he recognised the face of his enemy, Julian the governor.

Vengeance was in his grasp: 'an eye for an eye, a hand for a hand, a
tooth for a tooth'. He could overpower his enemy easily. . . . The poor
haggard wretch before him crept from the manger and fell on his
knees. . . . Marcus waited, and there was no sound in the stable but the
munching of the patient beasts that stood in their stalls.

He had believed he should see Christ on the earth. Was it to be . . . in
the manger . . . hanging on the cross, or the triumphant risen King
among the clouds of heaven? He knew . . . it was none of these but in that
emaciated form of his worst enemy God had shown himself to him.
And he took his enemy by the hand and raised him up and led him to his
own house.

And in this fashion Christ came once more upon the earth.

Beyond fame and fortune

The Story of George Washington Carver

Moses Carver, a hardworking Missouri farmer who was opposed to
slavery, had been forced by circumstances to buy Mary from a neighbour
to help his ailing wife and to be her companian whilst he toiled in the
fields. During the Civil War, raiders terrorised the area and kidnapped
slaves in order to sell them on further south for vastly inflated sums. One
night Mary and two of her children, one a sickly baby, were snatched.
Being an honest man, Moses Carver sought help to ransom them, and six
days later the sickly baby George was returned to him. He had been
given to some women who were told 'He ain't worth nothin'.

Throughout his childhood George caught every illness there was, but
somehow he survived each time. When the war ended, George, now a
free man, continued to live on the farm learning many less physically
demanding skills – how to knit and sew. He spent hours with insects and
beetles and learned to care for plants of all kinds with a special skill
which soon earned him a local reputation. He had an eye for colour and
shape and was soon painting pictures with primitive materials. His
greatest wish was to go to school, but being a negro there was no place
for him. George did not give up; he found a school for coloured children
in a nearby town where he enrolled and lived with a loving Christian
couple, Andrew and Mariah Watkins, who had no family of their own.
For the next ten years George moved from place to place, doing odd jobs
in order to earn enough to pay for his education and basic food. 'Give

him a good school, Lord,' Mariah Watkins had prayed when George left, 'because there's an awful lot that boy wants to know.'

When he finished school George applied to a college in Kansas, but on arriving to take up his place he was told 'Highland College does not take negroes'. Disillusioned, George went to work on the Kansas Plains where furious blizzards blew from the north in winter and in summer the corn shrivelled in the scorching winds. Gradually time healed his spirit and George began to read and paint again. With the help of kindly Christian people he gained a place at Simpson College, Iowa, where he studied etymology, composition, mathematics and (his greatest love) art. He moved on to Iowa Agricultural College and there was persuaded to enter some of his paintings in the Iowa Art Exhibition. So great was his success that the following year one of his paintings was shown at the World's Columbian Exposition in Chicago. But to George, the friendship and encouragement of his fellow students meant more than sudden fame.

In 1894, George received his Bachelor of Science degree and went to work as assistant to Dr. Louis Pammell, professor of Iowa University. He wrote articles for scientific journals and 1896 was awarded his M.A. At this time an eminent negro, Booker T. Washington, was struggling to set up a coloured people's institute of learning in Tuskagee, Alabama. He wrote to George offering no more than hard work and the opportunity for George to fulfil his longing to improve the lot of his own people. George accepted and set off with high hopes, but it was not long before he was to see the black faces devoid of any hope in the land where cotton was king. The land had been over-worked, the soil eroded and the people struggled to keep going despite decreasing crops. George began to establish his laboratory. He sent his students out to collect rusted pans, old bottles, wire, metal, anything that could be used as equipment. They reclaimed kitchen waste and made fertiliser, and surprisingly, instead of planting yet more cotton in their plots, George ordered them to sow Cowpeas, the only crop to feed nitrogen back into the soil instead of taking goodness out. They planted sweet potatoes and other vegetables and when eventually George did plant cotton, the ground yielded an unheard of 500 pound bales per acre.

The following years were productive and rewarding for George. The University developed, the grounds were landscaped, people came from miles around to seek advice and do research, but again and again, George stressed that only service counted, not money in the bank and clothes on one's back. The students began to broaden the school's curriculum, and George became the piano teacher, having learnt to play during his wanderings. The University was short of money, so George arranged a concert tour playing in big cities and small towns, and he raised a vast sum of money. During the tour he noticed the squalid homes of his people and he set about changing their lot. The Farmers' Institute was founded, and George visited isolated farming communities travelling by wagon and mule and carrying with him packets of seeds, tools and boxes of plants. He taught the farmers how to raise crops other than cotton, how to set aside money in order to buy their own smallholdings, and he taught the women how to cook the vegetables and how to flavour food with herbs. To the end of his life George felt this had been his most worthwhile achievement.

For years George had begged farmers to plant a variety of crops, but ironically it was the plague of boll weevil that finally forced them to listen. He persuaded farmers to plant a new little vine that produced a peanut. His campaign was so successful that many farmers faced disaster – their barns were full of surplus peanuts! George was tormented with guilt, but being the man he was, he set to work to find an answer to the problem. Seeking God's help he worked night and day and emerged from his laboratory with fats and gums, resins, sugars and starches which he had isolated from the peanut. He made hoards of synthetic materials – milk, ink, dyes, creosote, shoe polish and, of course, peanut butter. From the shells he made soil conditioners, fuels and a lightweight waterproof substance that looked like marble. Years later George Washington Carver was acknowledged as the world's first chemurgist (or agricultural chemist). By the end of the First World War the U.S. peanut industry was worth 80 million dollars with over 300 by-products: bleach, cheese, mayonnaise, linoleum, adhesives and many others.

After the death of Booker T Washington, his great mentor, George devoted himself to researching the use of agricultural products for things other than food and clothing. His synthetic marble led to the formation of the plastics industry; he devised products from the sweet potato and laid the groundwork for another vast industry – that of dehydrated foods which are in common use today. As a man of obvious scientific genius, any one of these discoveries could have made George Carver a wealthy man, but he even had to be reminded to cash his meagre pay cheque (he refused any increase on his original salary of 125 dollars a month from Booker T. Washington). Thomas Edison invited him to work in his laboratories for 100,000 dollars, but George declined the offer, refusing to claim rewards from gifts God had given, but gave instead the secrets of his discoveries to anyone who asked.

George Carver's reputation spread throughout the world. His paintings were acclaimed in many galleries but he gave his work away to any who admired it. Many rich and famous people sought his advice; he even advised Gandhi on his diet and suggested foodstuffs suitable for growing in India. Henry Ford was a frequent visitor and as a consequence of their friendship and work George extracted a milky substance from the golden rod plant which became a synthetic substitute for rubber.

During his fortieth year at Tuskagee an exhibition was staged to commemorate George's work. During his last years the George Carver Foundation was created to provide means for negro students. George died peacefully on January 20th. 1943, after a life of service, fortitude, dedication and faith. This simple epitaph appears on his grave:

He could have added fortune to fame, but caring for neither, he found happiness and honour in being helpful to the world.

'Well?'

G. A. Studdert Kennedy's *Rough Rhymes of a Padre* moved the hearts of thousands of people in the First World War. They said for the soldiers the things they wanted to say for themselves, and brought home the truth to the people left in England.

His dialect poems were written to be spoken in a cockney accent as by an uneducated but admirably resilient British soldier enduring the hell of the First World War in the trenches of Flanders.

> Our Padre was a solemn bloke,
>   We called 'im dismal Jim,
> It fairly gave ye t' bloomin' creeps,
>   To sit and 'ark at 'im,
> When'e were on wi' Judgment Day,
>   Abaht that great white throne,
> And 'ow each chap would 'ave to stand,
>   And answer on 'is own.
> And if 'e tried to charnce 'is arm,
>   And 'ide a single sin,
> There'd be the angel Gabriel,
>   Wi' books to do 'im in.
> 'E 'ad it all writ dahn, 'e said,
>   And nothin' could be 'id,
> 'E 'ad it all i' black and white,
>   And 'e would take no kid.
> And every single idle word,
>   A soldier charnced to say,
> 'E'd 'ave it all thrown back at 'im,
>   I' court on Judgment Day.
> Well I kep' mindin' Billy Briggs,
>   A pal o' mine what died.

'E went to 'elp our sergeant Smith,
    But as 'e reached 'is side,
There came and bust atween 'is legs,
    A big Boche 5.9 pill.
And I picked up 'is corpril's stripes,
    That's all there were o' Bill.
I called to mind a stinkin' night
    When we was carryin' tea.
We went round there by Limerick Lane,
    And Bill were a'ead o' me.
'Twere rainin' 'eavens 'ard, ye know,
    And t' boards were thick wi' muck,
And umpteen times we slithered dahn,
    And got the dicksee stuck.
Well, when we got there by the switch,
    A loose board tipped right up,
And Bill, 'e turned a somersault,
    And dahn 'e came, and whup!
I've 'eard men blind, I've 'eard 'em cuss,
    And I've 'eard 'em do it 'ard;
Well, 'aven't I 'eard our R.S.M.,
    Inspectin' special guard!
But Bill, 'e left 'im standin' still.
    'E turned the black night blue,
And I guess the angel Gabriel
    'Ad short 'and work to do.
Well, 'ow would poor old Bill go on,
    When 'e stood all alone,
And 'ad to 'ear that tale read out
    Afore the great white throne?
If what our Padre says is right,
    'E'd 'ave a rotten spell,
And finish up uv it, I s'pose,
    'E'd 'ave to go to 'ell.
And yet 'e were a decent lad,
    And met a decent end;
You'll never finish decenter,
    Than tryin' to 'elp a friend.
But some'ow I can't think it's right,
    It ain't what God would do.
This stunt of all these record books,
    I think it's all napoo,
'Twould let some rotten beggars in,

And keep some good 'uns out,
There's lots o' blokes, what does no wrong,
   As can't do nowt but shout.
But t'other night I dreamed a dream,
   And, just 'twixt me and you,
I never dreamed like that afore;
   I 'arf thinks it were true.
I dreamed as I were dead, ye see,
   At least as I 'ad died,
For I were very much alive,
   Out there on t'other side.
I couldn't see no judgment court,
   Nor yet that white great throne,
I couldn't see no record books,
   I seemed to stand alone,
I seemed to stand alone, beside
   A solemn kind o' sea.
Its waves they got in my inside,
   And touched my memory,
And day by day, and year by year,
   My life came back to me.
I seed just what I were, and what
   I'd 'ad the charnce to be.
And all the good I might 'a' done,
   And 'adn't stopped to do.
I seed I'd made an 'ash of it,
   And Gawd! but it were true.
A throng o' faces came and went,
   Afore me on that shore,
My wife, and mother, kiddies, pals,
   And the face of a London whore.
And some were sweet, and some was sad,
   And some put me to shame,
For the dirty things I'd done to 'em,
   When I 'adn't played the game.
Then in the silence some one stirred,
   Like when a sick man groans,
And a kind o' shivering chill ran through
   The marrer uv my bones.
And there before me someone stood,
   Just lookin' dahn at me,
And still be'ind 'im moaned and moaned
   That everlastin' sea.

I couldn't speak, I felt as though
   'E 'ad me by the throat,
'Twere like a drownin' fellah feels,
   Last moment 'e's afloat.
And 'e said nowt, 'e just stood still
   For I dunno 'ow long.
It seemed to me like years and years,
   But time out there's all wrong.
'What was 'e like?' you're askin' now.
   Can't word it anyway.
'E just were 'im, that's all I knows.
   There's things as words can't say.
It seemed to me as though 'is face
   Were millions rolled in one;
It never changed yet always changed,
   Like the sea beneath the sun.
'Twere all men's face yet no man's face,
   And a face no man can see,
And it seemed to say in silent speech,
   'Ye did 'em all to me.
The dirty things ye did to 'em,
   The filth ye thought was fine,
Ye did 'em all to me,' it said,
   'For all their souls were mine.'
All eyes were in 'is eyes – all eyes,
   My wife's and a million more;
And once I thought as those two eyes
   Were the eyes of the London whore.
And they was sad – my Gawd, 'ow sad,
   Wiv tears what seemed to shine,
And quivering bright wi' the speech o' light
   They said, 'Er soul was mine.'
And then at last 'e said one word,
   'E just said one word– 'Well?'
And I said in a funny voice,
   'Please can I go to 'ell?'
And 'e stood there and looked at me,
   And 'e kind o' seemed to grow,
Till 'e shone like the sun above my 'ead,
   And then 'e answered 'No,
You can't, for 'ell is for the blind,
   And not for those that see.
You know that you 'ave earned it, lad,

So you must follow me.
Follow me on by the paths o' pain,
  Seeking what you 'ave seen,
Until at last you can build the "Is"
  Wi' the brick o' the "Might 'ave been".'
That's what 'e said, as I'm alive,
  And that there dream were true.
But what 'e meant – I don't quite know,
  Though I knows what I 'as to do.
I's got to follow what I's seen,
  Till this old carcass dies;
For I daren't face in the land o' grace
  The sorrow o' those eyes.
There ain't no throne, and there ain't no books,
  It's 'im you've got to see,
It's 'im, just 'im, that is the judge
  Of blokes like you and me.
And, boys, I'd sooner frizzle up,
  I' the flames of a burnin' 'ell,
Than stand and look into 'is face,
  And 'ear 'is voice say – 'Well?'

The coming of the King

A story for Epiphany-tide by Laura E. Richards

Some children were at play in their playground one day, when a herald rode through the town, blowing a trumpet, and crying aloud, 'The King! The King passes by this road today. Make ready for the King!' The children stopped their play, and looked at one another. 'Did you hear that?' they said. 'The King is coming. He may look over the wall and see our playground; who knows? We must put it in order.'

The playground was sadly dirty, and in the corners were scraps of paper and broken toys, for these were careless children. But now, one brought a hoe, and another a rake, and a third ran to fetch the wheelbarrow from behind the garden gate. They laboured hard, till at length all was clean and tidy.

'Now it is clean!' they said; 'but we must make it pretty, too, for kings are used to fine things; maybe he would not notice mere cleanness, for he may have it all the time.'

Then one brought sweet rushes and strewed them on the ground; and others made garlands of oak leaves and fine tassels and hung them on the walls; and the littlest one pulled marigold buds and threw them all about the playground, 'to look like gold', he said.

When all was done the playground was so beautiful that the children stood and looked at it, and clapped their hands with pleasure.

'Let us keep it always like this,' said the littlest one; and the others cried, 'Yes! Yes! that is what we will do.'

They waited all day for the coming of the King, but he never came; only, towards sunset, a man with travel-worn clothes, and a kind, tired face passed along the road, then stopped to look over the wall.

'What a pleasant place!' said the man. 'May I come in and rest, dear children?'

The children brought him in gladly, and set him on the seat that they had made out of an old cask. They had covered it with the old red cloak to make it look like a throne, and it made a very good one.

'It is our playground,' they said. 'We made it pretty for the King, but he did not come, and now we mean to keep it so for ourselves.'

'That is good!' said the man.

'Because we think pretty and clean is nicer than ugly and dirty!' said another.

'That is better!' said the man.

'And for tired people to rest in!' said the littlest one.

'That is best of all!' said the man.

He sat and rested, and looked at the children with such kind eyes that they came about him and told him all they knew; about the five puppies in the barn, and the thrush's nest with four blue eggs, and the shore where the gold shells grew; and the man nodded and understood all about it.

By and by he asked for a cup of water, and they brought it to him in the best cup, with the gold sprigs on it; then he thanked the children, and rose and went on his way; but before he went he laid his hand on their heads for a moment, and the touch went warm to their hearts. The children stood by the wall and watched the man as he went slowly along. The sun was setting, and the light fell in long slanting rays across the road.

'He looks so tired!' said one of the children.

'But he was so kind!' said another.

'See!' said the littlest one. 'How the sun shines on his hair! It looks like a crown of gold.'

Homecoming

'Good to have you back, son,'
the old man said.
'Nice to be back.'
'You've had a rough time.'
The eyes clouded with
guilt. 'Hope you don't think
I let you down.'
The younger shook his head.
'You warned me, dad. But
it wasn't the nails.
It was the kiss.'
[Roger Woddis]

The story of two camels

by Frank Cooke

Once upon a time there were two camels. One was called Dan, who had
the nickname Dan the Doer because in everything he said 'I can, so I
will.'

He had great humps on his back which enabled him to travel miles
further than other beasts of burden who needed to stop for food and
water. He could so he did. He also noticed that he had large spongy feet
which spread out as he walked, enabling him to tread easily over loose
sand and thus to walk where other beasts would sink deeply into the soft
surface. He could so he did!

He also had thick pads on his knees which made kneeling down easy.
Now camels that don't kneel are not a lot of help because they are too tall
to load or climb on. Dan said 'I can so I will' and in all these things he
enjoyed being what he was and used his special camel-gifts to help
everyone he met. Dan was a good and happy camel.

The other camel was called Willie, who had the name Willie the Wisher
because he was always wanting to be something else, somewhere else,
doing something else. He lived in a zoo and one day seemed to know
that it was a special 'wishing day' and his every wish would come true. It
was like a dream.

He wished he could walk round the zoo and not be noticed, and
suddenly it happened and round the zoo he walked looking at the other
animals. When he saw the elephant he said, 'Oh, I wish I had a trunk like
that' and immediately he became a camelephant. He wandered round

214

the next area of the zoo and saw an antelope flowing gracefully over the grass. 'Oh, I wish I was like that' he said and instantly he became a camelephantelope. Next door were the pelicans being fed with fish. 'I love fish. I wish I could swallow them like that' and bang! He became a camelephantelopelican.

He stood under a tree to rest and heard a canary singing and wished he could sing like that, and instantly he became a camelephantelopelicanary.

That's the story. Now there are three things to do:

(1) Say it with me, after 'three':
    One, two, three – camelephantelopelicanary.
(2) If you can't say it, draw it and we will have a display of the best pictures.
(3) Remember, it's not about camels at all. It's all about people just like us!

The pulley

> When God at first made Man,
> Having a glass of blessings standing by,
> 'Let us,' said he, 'pour on him all we can;
> Let the world's riches, which dispersèd lie,
>   Contract into a span.'
>
> So strength first made a way,
> Then beauty flowed, then wisdom, honour, pleasure;
> When almost all was out, God made a stay,
> Perceiving that, alone of all his treasure,
>   Rest in the bottom lay.
>
> 'For if I should,' said he,
> 'Bestow this jewel also on my creature,
> He would adore my gifts instead of me,
> And rest in Nature, not the God of Nature:
>   So both should losers be.
>
> 'Yet let him keep the rest,
> But keep them with repining restlessness;
> Let him be rich and weary, that at least,
> If goodness lead him not, yet weariness
>   May toss him to my breast.'

[George Herbert]

Bible references

Useful addresses

Action on Smoking and Health (ASH)
5–11 Mortimer Street
London WIN 7RH
(01 637 9843)

British Astronomical Association
Burlington House
Piccadilly
London WIV ONL
(01 734 4145)

The British Safety Council
62–64 Chancellors Road
London W6 9RS
(01 741 1231)

Christian Aid
P.O.Box 1
London SW9 8BH
(01-733 5500)

Fact & Faith Films
120 The Rock
Bury
Lancashire BL9 OPJ
(061 764 1538)

The Health Education Council
78 New Oxford Street
London WCIA IAH
(01 637 1881)

International Boys Town Trust
50 Willesden Avenue
Walton
Peterborough PE4 6EA
(0733 76597)

Madame Tussaud's and the London
Planetarium
Marylebone Road
London NW1 5LR
(01 935 6861)

OXFAM
274 Banbury Road
Oxford OX2 7DZ
(0865 56777)

Religious and Moral Education Press
Hennock Road
Exeter
Devon EX2 8RP
(0392 74121)

The Old Royal Observatory
The National Maritime Museum
Greenwich Park
London SE10
(01 858 4422)

The Save the Children Fund
Mary Datchelor House
17 Grove Lane
London SE5 8RD
(01-703 5400)

TEAR Fund
11 Station Road
Teddington
Middx TW11 9AA
(01 977 9144)

Hymn index

* in the index indicates hymns which do not appear in strictly alphabetical order in the Teachers Music Book.

Acknowledgements

We are grateful to the following for permission to reproduce copyright material:

BBC Enterprises Ltd for a prayer from p 68 *New Every Morning* (revised edition, 1955); the author's agents for poems from pp 94 & 165 *Collected Poems* by Charles Causley (pub Macmillan); James Clarke and Co Ltd for 'The Coming of The King' by Laura Richards; William Collins Sons & Co Ltd for an extract from p 111 *The Screwtape Letters* by C S Lewis; The Daily Telegraph Ltd for the poem 'Homecoming' by Roger Woddis from p 253 *Book of Mini-Sagas* ed Brian Aldiss (pub Alan Sutton Publishing Ltd, 1985) Copyright Telegraph Sunday Magazine; Epworth Press for extracts from p 27 & 368 *Daily Readings From W E Sangster* ed Frank Cumbers Copyright Frank Cumbers; Faber and Faber Ltd for Section IV from 'Little Gidding' in *Four Quartets* by T S Eliot and the poem 'The Killing' from *The Collected Poems of Edwin Muir* by Edwin Muir; Gill and Macmillan Ltd for the poem 'Lord, I have time' from pp 76–78 *Prayers of Life* by Michel Quoist; Hodder & Stoughton Ltd for an extract from pp 121–122 *God in Man's Experience* by L Griffith and an extract from p 301 *I Believe in The Church* by David Watson (pub Hodder, 1978); the author's agents for 'The Story of Weaver' by William James and Richard Weaver in *Varieties of Religious Experience* by William James; the author, Phyllis McCormack for her poem 'Look Closer'; John Murray (Publishers) Ltd for the poem 'Christmas' from *Collected Poems* by John Betjeman (pub John Murray, 1979); the author's agents for an extract from *An Only Child* by Frank O'Connor (pub Macmillan); The Putnam Publishing Group for a poem by W. H. Carruth from p 33 *Youth at Worship* ed G S Pain (pub Methodist Youth Dept, 1934); The Royal Literary Fund for a poem by Eden Phillpotts; Dr Paul Sangster and Epworth Press for extracts from pp 10, 24, 144, 147 *Westminster Sermons* Vol 2 ed W E Sangster; SCM Press Ltd for the story of the White Birds from p 9 *The School of Prayer* by Olive Wyon (pub SCM Press, 1943); Sidgwick & Jackson for a poem by L Houseman from p 38 *Youth at Worship* (pub Methodist Youth Dept, 1934); The Society of Authors as the Literary representative of the Estate of John Masefield for an extract from *The Everlasting Mercy* by John Masefield; Stainer and Bell Ltd for the poem 'You who are 17' from *The Two-Way Clock* by Sydney Carter Copyright Sydney Carter.

We have been unable to trace the author of the book *Heaven's Alive,* Dr Roger Pilkington, or the copyright holder in the poem 'What is real' by M Williams Bianco from p 34 *Worship and Wonder* (pub Galliard, 1971) and would appreciate any information that would enable us to do so.

Cover photograph by Pictorial Press